The Irish and the Blank Page

"... a well documented, very readable volume."
—Ken Blue, Author of *Healing Spiritual Abuse*

HOW ANCIENT CELTS TEACH US THE NEW COVENANT

ROGER SCHMIDT

© 2012 by Roger Schmidt. All rights reserved.
2nd Printing 2014

Trusted Books is an imprint of Deep River Books. The views expressed or implied in this work are those of the author. To learn more about Deep River Books, go online to www.DeepRiverBooks.com.

No part of this publication may be reproduced, stored in a retrieval system, or transmitted in any way by any means—electronic, mechanical, photocopy, recording, or otherwise—without the prior permission of the copyright holder, except as provided by USA copyright law.

Unless otherwise noted, all Scriptures are taken from the *Holy Bible, New International Version*®, *NIV*®. Copyright © 1973, 1978, 1984 by Biblica, Inc.™ Used by permission of Zondervan. All rights reserved worldwide. www.zondervan.com

ISBN 13: 978-1-63269-189-7
Library of Congress Catalog Card Number: 2011932296

For Zoe, Aaron and Audrey

Contents

1. Discovering the Irish Story 1
2. The Celts 13
3. Newness with a Skeleton 33
4. Features of the New 45
5. Patrick 57
6. Similarities Between Us and the Irish 71
7. Early Irish Characteristics 93
8. Rejuvenating Ancient Traits 113
9. The Next Step 129

Conclusion 143

Endnotes 147

Appendix 153

CHAPTER 1

Discovering the Irish Story

THE NEW COVENANT took hold of my thoughts one November evening in 1995. I was living in San Francisco on a short-term work assignment and making the most of being an expatriate. One of my more satisfying discoveries was a vibrant neighborhood bookstore that regularly featured guest authors. That November evening, ex-Doubleday publisher turned historian Thomas Cahill was the visiting author. Cahill, as I would later learn, has a wide-ranging theological and philosophical education that includes ability to read in a number of ancient and modern languages. He applied his skills then, and now, at studying pivotal periods of history. Staff had pushed bookshelves to the corners and set up folding chairs to accommodate the crowd. Most were casually dressed, looking as though they had walked from the nearby townhouses of Larkspur Landing or driven from adjacent Tiburon or San Rafael. I had walked down the winding road from our townhome, managed to grab a chair, and felt no small amount of gratitude for this bookstore that regularly attracted such prominent authors. Cahill was promoting his new book *How the Irish Saved Civilization*, and began by reading excerpts from the ancient epic saga the *Táin Bó Cúailnge,* describing Irish affectations, such as the "green and white martyrs."

The Irish and the Blank Page

As the evening continued, I found myself captivated by the thought of the fifth-century Irish and how they transformed from what some would call "savages" into saints and scholars in just one century. As I walked back up the hill to our townhouse with a copy of Cahill's book under my arm, I sensed that if the stories I had heard were even partly true, I had stumbled on something unique. The Irish transformation was not only astoundingly fast, but the way they expressed their Christianity seemed so free, and so authentic. Their experience of the gospel was so heartfelt and intense that it made my own experience seem pale. Further, the effect of the gospel was not limited to a collection of individuals; it transformed the entire culture. For some reason, Christianity was delivered to the Irish in a way that produced a speedy, thorough, and lasting transformation—a transformation that, in hindsight, they still consider positive, that continues to inspire people, and that they could not contain to their own shores.

Apparently, the Irish had ingested the best of what we call the gospel, wrapped it around their culture, and allowed it to permeate their hearts so that it enhanced every part of their lives. They were so enthusiastic about their new lives that they took their transformational experience on the road and rejuvenated most of western Europe. The appeal of their story was undeniable and their experience and its place in history seemed too important not to investigate further.

I studied Cahill's book and could not get it out of my mind. For those like me, who had been led to follow Jesus in ways that seemed designed to produce conformance of lifestyle rather than enhancement of lives, the Irish story was a marker. The Irish saw religious instruction and experience as the ultimate gift, while I often see it as stale, repetitive, and forced. The Irish conversion was not coerced; they did not have to receive ongoing apologies from the church for acts of cultural suffocation. Their kids were not shuffled into residential schools. Rather, they connected with Christianity in a way that saw their native art flourish and they saw themselves transform to become instruments of positive, intellectual, and spiritual change for neighboring countries and regions. They literally did save civilization by copying and protecting manuscripts and re-evangelizing western Europe after Rome retreated. I wanted more of what they had.

I had many questions. Why the Irish? Why did they so uniquely connect with the faith? Was the story I heard accurate? I wanted to dig into the details of past Irish exploits and learn about their robust simplicity, but my search was only partly a historical quest. The primary motivation for my search was that their enthusiasm seemed like just the tonic for the dreary faith that I have often experienced and is often packaged as normal fare.

I am Canadian, not Irish. My pre-Canadian heritage is mostly German and partly Dutch. I come from relatively simple roots. My parents were raised on family farms: my dad in the Ukraine and my mom in the central plains of Canada. Both left that direct connection with the land, met in Saskatoon, where my dad was studying engineering, and settled in Vancouver. They raised me with a sense of community, an appreciation for home cooking, and a belief in God. God was such a part of the fabric of our household that making a decision to follow him was natural. And I did. My spiritual roots were tended in a few denominations, including Mennonite Brethren, Vineyard, and Pentecostal. I will discuss relevant parts of my background in later chapters, but what became a bigger challenge than deciding to follow God was continuing to believe he was good and relevant.

In my world, religion was rarely discussed as something trivial or irrelevant, but it was also rarely experienced as something that was vibrant and expansive and visibly transformative. In my youth, our religious routine consisted of Sunday morning and evening sermons and fireside room meetings. I knew that atmosphere with as much intimacy as the Irish knew tales of battle and communed with nature. The sights and smells of the church were as familiar to me as those of my own house. I remember the cold and damp feel of the lobby when we would arrive at church early, and I remember the silhouette of my mother talking to another lady in front of the last lit window while we sat in the car with my dad, waiting to go home. For me the church was a meeting spot, community center, sports complex, and house of faith. Church formed the biggest part of my early life. But no one I knew traveled to craggy islands in the sea like the Skellig Rocks in County Kerry, where Celtic monks made homesteads and lived for centuries communing with God and nature. I didn't come across those who traveled beyond the realms of normal navigation like St. Brendan for the sake of their beliefs. My experience of prayer was detached from both the initial savagery and the final passion of the Irish.

Instead of that kind of vibrancy, my journey led me through the system, provided me religious education, subjected me to countless sermons, and placed me in numerous Bible studies. I was bathed in measured concepts and had every question answered before it had a chance to germinate in my mind. I was instructed to pursue balance. Celtic Christianity seemed just the prescription to inject some life into my spirituality.

The first question I had to ask was whether the Irish story was, in fact, too good to be true. History and its interpretation can be surprisingly subjective and my early enthusiasm was often muted by chords of inner doubt. Much of that doubt came from wanting to be critical and sophisticated—and I use the latter term in a negative sense. It was difficult for me to believe God is so profoundly good and that his program, the gospel, produces such thorough good in lives and cultures. I so often seem to hear otherwise. I hear about the church struggling against the odds, against the tide of evil. Or I hear about the overbearing church imposing culture, theology, and lifestyles on people too unsophisticated to resist. A tale of gospel transformation communicated by simple people using little coercion and involving dramatic success seems so stark by contrast as to almost be unbelievable.

Another concern looming less large—but, nevertheless, lurking in my mind—was why a story of such importance would be made so evident in one culture and in one specific century. Why was this type of experience not more common? That question resolved fairly quickly, as I know that truth is often selective. We could also ask why it was just one person, Newton, who discovered gravity, or why Jesus was born in a simple Jewish village in the first century.

We seem to always have a choice to recognize and study what has occurred or to question its validity and dismiss it as anomaly.

Regardless of which questions I asked, the answers always seemed to reveal more substance to the story. I read every primary historical account of St. Patrick I could find, made my own pilgrimage to Ireland to travel the land on which the stories had occurred, and even performed experiments of my own to test the story. It was not enough for me to read about St. Fridolin, "the traveler," the son of an Irish king who evangelized Thuringia. I emailed a friend I met in Leipzig who now lives in a village near Frankfurt and asked the generalized question (without preamble): "Tell me about the history of your town." He sent a brief note back saying he wasn't aware of much of the town history, but there was a statue of an Irish man in the town square. The physicality of things like that statue helped validate the story in my mind; and it seemed that wherever I looked, the Irish story was similarly validated. It was waiting to be uncovered; and once uncovered, the story was undeniable. The ongoing influence of the Irish seemed inescapable. Further investigations convinced me that the Irish had stumbled onto what might be called the unfettered version of the gospel—one that we were all meant to experience.

Why Did the Gospel Affect the Irish With Such Force?

Cahill had eloquently described the context and the significance of the Irish experience, but for me, something remained left to explore. I wanted to know why it happened and whether it could happen again. To answer those questions, I needed to understand what made the gospel affect the Irish with such force. Perhaps it was something about the fifth-century environment—it was a unique period of time that featured the decline of Roman influence, a marked decrease in political stability, and the retreat of the organized church to safer lands. It may have been something about the man who delivered the gospel to the Irish. Patrick is easily lost amidst the modern celebrations and shamrocks, yet he was a real person—a moderately educated man with motivation based in personal experience with God, rather than obligation to him. He was definitely passionate.

Perhaps it was his delivery that made the light of the gospel transparent to the Irish. Or maybe it was something about the ancient Celtic peoples themselves: their warlike, yet spiritual nature. They may have been savages, but they had a surprising level of sophistication and cultural development. The Irish placed a very high value on words. They believed that the center of the universe contained a core of truth that could be expressed in a single word. They had a mystical belief in the power of words and had a reverence for the way pure words could contain a level of power. They believed in the power of words and truth (both as blessings and curses) to alter the courses of lives. It was perhaps because of this that the Irish were able to ingest the Word of God, the Logos of God, as an integral word for them and their culture. The question I had was, "What amongst these various factors combined to create the Irish transformation?"

The historical factors are interesting and worth exploring. Much of the journey of this book is also tied to my own journey. It starts with a desire for more spiritual reality and a theory that what the Celts experienced points the way to that experience. It also contains a hunch that the "newness" of the gospel is a necessary ingredient to understand. The goal in the exploration then is to develop a template; to describe an example from which to move forward. This example is useful for myself and for others like me who seem trapped in a dreary religious existence or have shunned religion because they perceive (or recognize) that it produces little transformation or life.

I enjoy history but am also very practical. In order for me to consider the exploits of the Irish after Patrick worth studying, they had to be more than an historical anomaly. I needed to consider them a signpost that indicates the gospel can thrive in ways we can hardly imagine. The early Irish experience communicates a vibrancy to the gospel that was both uncommon and yet possible at the same time. It provides an example—a piece of data—that validates the superlative terminology we hear in church. And if the story provides one piece of data, then it also provides more. It seems the whole story was somehow staged, like a cultural science experiment in which many of the distracting variables were removed in order to highlight the important variable.

We will look at which variables were isolated, but what is interesting is that this cultural experiment, after having run its course for over 200 years, was validated by none other than the Roman church. There was a period of relative isolation in the Celtic church, and while there was some ongoing contact with Rome, it took some time for Roman clerics to regroup after the fall of the Roman Empire and formally make their way back to Britain. They first did so formally at the Synod of Whitby in 664. The Romans assessed their Celtic brethren and, incredibly, found only two differences over which to dispute. The correct date for Easter and the type of haircuts (or tonsure) the monks sported. The Irish eventually gave in on both issues—which was at least partly positive since the Celtic tonsure was something of a monastic mullet. But amazingly, over 200 years of Celtic Christianity had produced no significant mutations. Haircuts aside, the Celtic Christians did not display characteristics or beliefs that were contemptible to Roman Christians. Apparently, something was at work here that was not only full of life, but it was also robust and self-correcting.

The Celtic Christians seemed able to pave a more mystical and positive expression of the faith—an expression similar, yet distinct, from other flavors of Christianity at the time whether Roman or Eastern Orthodox. Granted, the Celtic Christians faced different opponents and found themselves in less threatening environments than Roman Christians did, but the fifth-century Irish story seemed poised to teach whoever is willing to listen that there really is more to the kingdom of God than battling heretics. There is a robust simplicity at the heart of the gospel—one that can awaken and enliven the heart of humanity.

Perhaps, like mine, the religious life you participate in produces little flourishing art and little passionate response. Certainly, mine is nothing akin to the passion of the green martyrs—those fifth-century Irish converts who regretted they had no persecutors

The Irish and the Blank Page

like the early church martyrs did, so they chose to express their dedication voluntarily by leaving their place of ultimate comfort, which included the social connection of the towns and villages to pursue God in the green (the wild).

These were spiritually passionate and slightly odd figures such as St. Kevin, who retreated to the valley of two lakes (Glendalough) and hid himself in the holes and crevices of the rock walls surrounding the lakes in order to both avoid people and commune with God. He was a hermit and it was not his social traits that attracted followers, but nevertheless they materialized. One day, God spoke to Kevin, who was living in the rocks above the lake, and said, "Go down to the valley and start a monastery." Which he did. The monastery flourished and still stands today. Kevin led the monastic community, but always preferred connection with nature and God. He would regularly pray in the early morning while standing in the cold water of the smaller lake.

Trying to reconcile acts of Irish passion (like Kevin's) with my religious experience required me to first recognize differences. Their exposure to, and reception of, the gospel differed largely from mine. It produced different results, it was more intense, it was more visible, and it was more enhancing.

There is a thread of similarity. Thankfully, my spiritual journey, even though tracked through some stale church environments, included one environment that allowed me to connect with the substance of the gospel. Like the Irish, that connection changed my life. It changed what felt like a world shaded in tones of black and white to a world bathed in color. I came to know the God who kicks the doors of a life open wide and not only leaves the old room in shambles, but presents new possibilities and adventures. So, for me, as with the Irish, there was an environment and a presentation of the gospel that caused the singular truth of it to resonate in my heart in an authentic and life-changing way.

But what seems apparent is that, except for a few brief interludes, the bulk of my church experience has not occurred in that environment. More of it has occurred in the environment of routine and low expectations. An environment in which, for the most part, transformation is rare. We heard exciting stories from abroad; however, at home, people with problems keep their problems to themselves. We did have converts, but they were few. Like the Irish, the immediacy and emotion of their salvation had a welcome effect on the community, but those new believers often seem like a strange breed. I would wonder what brought them to our sheltered hideaway, where we mostly were concerned with staying safe from the evils of false beliefs and the world.

While the bulk of my church environment has displayed a few indicators of life—indicators that suggest the Irish experience was of the same nature as ours—there were also plenty of signs that it was different. Our experience of the gospel was muted, strained, and paler. Apparently we used what seems like the same religious language but, judging by the experience that followed, there was something different about how we understood, interpreted, or received the words.

If the experience of passion is related to the words that were communicated, then there must have been something different about the words they used or how they used them. The Irish valued words as powerful and spiritual—and my church used words in a careless sense. When people in my church were taking words seriously, they used words like tools for the purpose of reinforcing and defending their beliefs. Words like *pagan, atheist, unbeliever, infidel,* and even *liberal* were used to label outsiders and protect us from "them."

Primarily, the start of knowledge is to recognize what you don't know. I had to recognize that the Irish had what I had largely missed and now wanted more of: something that similarly inspires my passion.

I wanted to dig into the Irish story to understand the ingredients that fueled their passion, but I was also motivated by a desire to make sense of my mission. The Irish did not keep their new lives to themselves. It seems that would have been impossible. Irish lives spilled over the edges of their island and they voluntarily reached out to the world around them. They did this with astounding success. Jesus left his followers the task of going into the world and making disciples, yet in our time and in my mind that task has often been described as "proselytizing." It's become, to me, a horrible word, one that makes our primary task seem manipulative, shameful, and even inhuman. Many people feel that the gospel never really had anything to offer for humanity (only for the afterlife) and what benefit it may have had in the past has somehow expired in our postmodern world. Yet the Irish experience shows that mission work can be performed in the daylight—with truly honorable results—from many perspectives. If there is a design to the Irish story, then one lesson it teaches is that something at the heart of the gospel almost explodes and doesn't need to be managed; it just needs to be released. If only we would find the nerve or the will to let it out more often.

Reasons to Study

Perhaps, your spiritual passion is also flagging or, perhaps, it has never really ignited. Maybe you need to make further sense of your involvement in the church or in your ongoing missionary endeavors. Maybe you have wondered about the things we do in the place we call church and the way we follow God. Does it really represent our faith well? When you look over the religious scenery that surrounds you—that you have chosen—maybe it appears gray, stale, and lifeless. I'd like to expect vitality, real community, and power to change rather than just words that describe those realities. If you haven't given up on those aspirations, I encourage you to read on and join in the discovery of the things that can reenergize your spiritual life and enable you to experience and communicate the gospel with sincerity and passion.

How We Will Proceed

We will look at the Irish through historical documents. Like any historical documents, some are better than others. In the case of early Christian Ireland, many have been embellished by the legend surrounding St. Patrick, but there are primary and trustworthy documents, some written by Patrick himself. What seems most indelibly left as a record for our review is the Irish themselves, and their deeds, of which evidence and records still remain. Often what's left in the documents is not so much stark evidence but, rather, clues and hints that force us to deduce the way the gospel was presented by Patrick and received by the Irish.

To make sense of the clues and hints, we will start our exploration into the reasons for their success with one assumption. A hypothesis, if you will. Many experiments begin this way—with a hunch. It helps focus the study, isolate the variables, and move forward. My reflection on the Irish experience has led me to believe there are critical words that explain their passion and allow it to be understood today. They are the words mentioned earlier, the words that took hold of my thoughts after hearing about the Irish in the bookstore, the Bible words, "new covenant." My hypothesis: the Irish connected deeply with what these two words represent. They are familiar words to any who inhabit church, yet they are also full of mostly undiscovered meaning and implication. They speak of the new architecture that God designed for our relationship with him—a structure that makes all previous ones redundant. It's the new operating system. We will define the new covenant in some detail and see the territory it encompasses is truly vast. Within that vast territory fits the story of the fifth-century Irish. Their story will be used to illuminate and amplify these words. To confirm our hypothesis we will see how the Irish connected with each of the salient features of the new covenant.

The gospel, as described in the new covenant, was something that was barrier-free to the Irish and fit with their culture. For us, in the religious west, the opposite is true. The new covenant (the heart of the gospel) is behind cultural barriers, it often does not fit with our expectations, and has largely been ignored. It was the new covenant that awakened the kind of productive passion that the Irish were privileged to experience over 1,500 years ago. To see how this happened, we will explore the Celts, and we will look at the primary features of the new covenant. Finally, beginning with Patrick, we will look at the links between the two.

All people are, or were, Aboriginals. We all come from somewhere and we can relate to our cultures, our ancestors and their connection to the land.

—Douglas Cardinal[1]

CHAPTER 2

THE CELTS

Origins

ON THE TWENTY-FIRST day of December—the winter solstice—a ray of sunlight arcs low across the winter sky and passes through a small opening squared off by rough-hewn stones and travels through a long earthen passageway until it finally reaches its yearly destination—a central room inside a massive burial mound. The room is so small and the event of such limited duration that you have to win the lottery held by the Brú na Bóinne Visitor Centre to see this light for yourself. If you do find yourself huddled in this central room at dawn in December, you, along with a few privileged others, will share the experience that early people did over five thousand years ago.

Passage mounds occur at other locations in Ireland but the mound at Newgrange is the most massive and is now registered as a world heritage site. The central chamber lies beneath an earthen mound over three meters high, circular in shape that covers over an acre of land. It was an impressive engineering feat for prehistoric peoples who spent most of their time gathering food and fuel for subsistence. It is a surprising feat for people who took little time to build lasting structures for themselves. Archaeologists estimate hundreds of ancient Irish peoples would have toiled for decades to move and arrange the massive stones that define the mound, and then taken more time to decorate the exterior with brilliant white stones.

Thousands of years later, in the days when Rome was a local republic, Greek philosophy was just beginning to germinate, and the Babylonians were destroying the last remnants of the nation of Israel, the territory we know today as western Europe was populated by descendants of those passage mound builders. They had learned to fabricate iron weapons and then to clear forests with those weapons. This was about the sixth century BC—the Iron Age—and their skills in metalworking and their unified culture allowed them to quickly dominate most of the area. By the third century BC, they had spread from their origins, which the Greeks considered to be the headwaters of the Danube and Rhine, across all of Europe from the Atlantic Ocean to the Black Sea. They occupied areas we now know as England, Scotland, Ireland, France, Germany, parts of Spain, Austria, and Romania. For three hundred years they were the dominant people group of Europe. Greeks called them Keltoi, and in our era we call them by the name Edward Lhuyd coined in the seventeenth century—Celts.[2]

The Celts were not a single nation. There were varieties: Irish, Welsh, Galatian, and Gaulish to name a few. Yet they shared a common identity resulting primarily from their common language. That language is now expressed in modern-day variations such as Irish, Scottish, Gaelic, Manx, and Welsh. They also had a well-developed culture, which we will investigate as we dig into the Celtic past.

We dig deep into that past because to understand how they changed, we need to first consider who the Irish were. The gospel of the new covenant is not an alien force that possesses random hosts. Rather, as we'll see, the Father of us all changes the direction of spiritual gravity so he can connect with his children and release us to fully be who we are. God doesn't connect with us on a superficial level—the part we represent to others on an application form or résumé. He connects with us at our core: the real us. So scratching the surface of their character will not suffice. We look for the core of the Irish, and to find it we need to investigate their past.

Celts expanded across Europe at the same time Rome was expanding across the Mediterranean and were the first of the prehistoric peoples north of the Alps whose names were known to the Greek and Roman world.[3] Romans considered Celts "a powerful people with a certain ethnic unity, occupying wide and clearly defined territories...possessed of internal political organization and formidable military strength."[4] The two cultures seemed destined to clash, and the first major encounter occurred when the Romans suffered an attack from the Celts in 390 BC. In that year, Celts from Gaul successfully entered the city of Rome and forced the inhabitants to pay a ransom in return for their retreat. It was a significant Celtic military accomplishment, one that would not be repeated by any other people or tribe for the next eight hundred years. Celtic raids also occurred in Greece, such as that on the sanctuary of Delphi in 279 BC.

Oddly, those early Gaulish warriors did not occupy the Roman city, rather they eventually settled into regions east, establishing the Celtic state of Galatia.[5] But Romans did not forget about the Celts. Celts remained a perceived threat to Roman stability and represented a real obstacle to Roman expansion. Julius Caesar, in the first century BC, hoping to expand his reputation and prevent further incursions into Rome, focused his sights on Gaul. He waged eight campaigns against the Celts there and finally overcame their resistance—but not before millions of Gaulish Celts had been killed. In about 50 BC Gaul was defeated and became part of the Roman Empire. Roman soldiers also moved into Britain, defeating Celts there and occupying most of its southern areas. Other Celtic tribes also fell to Rome, and by the late fourth century AD, Celts throughout Europe were a conquered people who had adopted Roman ways—whether in Galatia, Wales, or Gaul.

The Roman onslaught was formidable but not complete. In regions such as Gaul, Celtic ways were virtually subsumed to become Roman ways, but the Roman Empire had endless borders to defend and Roman armies often had other priorities preventing them from fully subduing all the regions they conquered in battle. In many outlying areas such as Britain, Roman establishment and rule was much less complete and was more like that of an occupying army. Rome also reached physical and logistical limitations. There is a story of a Roman commander named Agricola looking across the Irish Sea and assessing that the island could be taken and held with one legion.[6] That legion was never requested and so the people of Ireland as well as the Scottish Celts north of Hadrian's Wall—the remaining European native Celts—were left unconquered. They were those at the edge of the habitable world that had not been dominated.

By virtue of their location, more than anything, the Irish Celts "beyond which nobody lives"[7] managed to resist influence by Rome. They retained the privilege of being the last of the Celtic natives—an unreached and isolated people group who had the freedom to exercise their ancient ways. These native Celts stand as the last of a prehistoric culture and provide a unique insight into the European past. Greek and Roman civilization provides understanding of the roots of western philosophy, thought, and culture, but the Celts are in fact our earliest European ancestors. They reveal in us something less cerebral. In them we see not ancestors of our rationality, but our actual ancestors.

Celts in Gaul and Britain were conquered by Romans. Those Celts not conquered by Rome were eventually conquered by the Norse, Angles, and Saxons. To some extent Celts were assimilated into all those cultures. Some even say the Teutons were Celtic peoples. Thus if you, like me, can trace your ancestors back to Celtic, Saxon, Angle, or Norse cultures, the Celts, in many ways, represent your native tribe and your earliest heritage.

As I began to understand the Celts in their historical context, I realized my attraction to their story had deep roots. It was more than a study of an isolated people group's experience of the gospel. These people apparently were my people group. Celts represent the native European: the aboriginal within many of us. That blood link suggests their journey can reveal something essential about the gospel for me; it can have rich significance in terms of understanding my roots and earliest tendencies. Understanding their transformation may also help me connect to my own innate spirituality.

If you can also make ancestral connections to the Celts, their story will contain added layers of significance for you. If not, their story contains themes that are common to humanity: the joy of desires fulfilled and the freedom that comes when restrictions are lifted.

For all those reasons we will look at the ancient Celts. Because the Irish were the last remaining true native Celtic peoples, we'll look at the Irish Celts in particular.

To continue the study of ancient Celts it is helpful to recognize that much of what has been written about them appears contradictory. We will attempt to address that contradiction and be wary of over simplifying their culture or adopting stereotypes.

Savages

Romans considered Celts, particularly those living on the fringes of their empire, to be uncivilized savages. This perception of savagery arose for many reasons, one of which was the ferocity of Celtic warriors. They fought aggressively and fearlessly and their warriors were inspired by passion. Ancient Celtic epic tales like the *Táin Bó Cúalnge* or *The Tain*, the story of the epic cattle raid of Cooley, focus almost entirely on the field of battle and highlight feats of strength. They also include fantastic and exaggerated accounts of hulk-like transitions warriors underwent during battle. The exaggerated descriptions of physical distortion are almost beyond imagination and are the often recounted portions of *The Tain*. After elaborately dressing for battle and before getting into his chariot, the youthful hero of *The Tain*, Cú, changes so that he

> became horrible, many-shaped, strange and unrecognisable. His haunches shook about him like a tree in a current or a bulrush against a stream, every limb and every joint, every end and every member of him from head to foot. He performed a wild feat of contortion with his body inside his skin. His feet and his shins and his knees came to the back; his heels and his calves and his

hams came to the front. The sinews of his calves came on the front of his shins and each huge, round knot of them was as big as a warrior's fist. The sinews of his head were stretched to the nape of his neck and every huge, immeasurable, vast, incalculable round ball of them was as big as the head of a month-old child.[8]

The text of *The Tain* goes on to describe further distortions, such as describing the "loud beating of his heart against his ribs which was heard like the baying of a bloodhound."

Aristotle claimed that Celts feared nothing, neither earthquakes or waves.[9] Even their women would strike fear into the hearts of onlookers as Dio Cassius confirms. He writes this description as late as the first century AD of the queen of the Iceni, a Celtic tribe in eastern Britain.

She was huge of frame, terrifying of aspect, and with a harsh voice. A great mass of bright red hair fell to her knees. She wore a great twisted golden torq, and a tunic of many colours, over which was a thick mantle fastened by a brooch. Now she grasped a spear, to strike fear into all who watched her.[10]

They were fierce warriors but were also considered savages because of ancient Celtic practices that included going into battle naked—with the exception of a metal neck ornament called a torq. The famous statue of the Dying Gaul portrays just such a soldier. Another practice that would've added to their savage reputation was the way Celts would display their enemy's remains: "whenever a distinguished enemy was killed in battle they would cleave open his head, make a ball of the brains by mixing them with lime, which was then dried and preserved as a trophy of the warrior's valor."[11]

Their après battle practices contributed to the perception of them as savages, as did the Celts' lack of, or avoidance of, written language. For the most part they relied on an unwieldy system of markings called Ogham script for written records. It was a cumbersome and slow method of marking, taking great amounts of time to produce. For example, ten markings were required to indicate the letter "i" and a similar amount to indicate "r." Ogham markings available to us today are left in stone obelisks and these were certainly not produced rapidly. You couldn't post tweets on Twitter in Ogham. To modern perceptions as well as to Roman ones at the time, the script indicated a society that had little desire to record their findings and little desire to communicate with others.

The Greeks and Romans wrote about the methods the Celtic seers and prophets—known as druids—used in foretelling the future. Tacitus, the Roman historian and son-in-law of the general Agricola, said, "The Druids consult the gods in the palpating entrails of men."[12] Their carvings included fertility figures in lewd poses such as the sheelanagig—a commonly found stone female carving. Their kings were known to copulate with horses in inauguration ceremonies. Their culture was filled with taboos, restrictions, and superstitions.

Celts were kidnappers. Roman occupiers in Britain would suffer Irish guerilla raids on vulnerable ports and harbors. These raids were annoyances more than any serious military threat, but they would result in unsuspecting inhabitants being carried away to be made slaves, most never to be seen again.

They seemed to have a primary god, Lugh, but were pantheistic. Triplets are a recurring theme in religious depictions. Common gods between tribes numbered about thirty with that number swelling tenfold when including unique tribal gods. Like their predecessors who built the massive sun-focused passage mounds, Celts were sun worshipers. One archaeologist describes the subject of Celtic gods as fertile chaos.[13]

They were rural. Urban life was foreign and repugnant to the Irish, who did not establish towns. They had no formal currency and used a simple unit of barter based on their primary source of wealth—cattle. One unit of barter (a set) was equal to half a dairy cow.

All these traits fueled the Roman image of the Celts, and particularly the northern Celts (such as the Irish), as savages. They were a people outside the influence and beyond the understanding of Romans.

Cultured

Yet, Celtic culture was in many ways not as savage as the Romans perceived. Because the Celts left us virtually no written records, our knowledge of their early culture comes entirely from what we read of them from others or what we find in archaeological remains. Celtic culture, is thus in some ways shrouded in secrecy. Descriptions from others often come from their enemies and thus require some critical assessment.

Native Celtic society and culture was rich and unique. The uniqueness sprang from their separation from the civilizations of the Mediterranean. This was more than physical separation. Because Celtic peoples did not deal in written communication, the accumulated knowledge of the ancient world was a closed book to them. Likewise the history, the intellectual life, the mythology, the religious experience the eloquence and art of the formal speech of the Celts were little known to the Greeks and Romans.[14] In their isolation the Celts developed unique expressions, not the least of which is their spiral artwork forms that repeat with unsymmetric patterns and uniquely blend human and animal figures into the patterns.

The Celts also developed advanced skills in spoken language. Their lack of written records encouraged them to memorize any thought or idea worth saving, and to do this they had to communicate in a way that assisted others in memorizing. This necessitated development of considerable skill with language and oratory and caused Ireland to develop "a greater wealth of carefully preserved oral tradition...than any other people in Europe north of the Alps."[15] Their skill with language was recognized by their Roman conquerors in Gaul, who often employed Celtic instructors to teach their children oratory.

Their epic mythical tale, *The Tain*, is one the longest and most important of the Celtic oral traditions. The battle excerpt quoted earlier is a small part of the sweeping narrative, which, in its current recorded version, extends over one hundred pages. It begins with a king and queen leisurely reclining on their bed, discussing the benefits of knowing each other and comparing their various talents and possessions. They quickly move to a dispute over who has greater possessions, justifying their positions by describing various articles and animals. Being Irish, they eventually narrow their comparison to cattle—a bull actually. The king has a magnificent bull named Findbennach that the queen cannot match. They hear of an Ulster bull that can possibly best Findbennach and proceed to search for this bull, named Donn Cúailnge, whom they intend to borrow for comparison. The Ulstermen ultimately refuse to loan Donn Cúailnge, so the king and queen assemble armies against them. It's an intense yet whimsical saga with a subplot that describes a larger-than-life teenage hero, Cú Chullain, and his gory battle exploits. One of the unique features of the story is its descriptions are surprisingly short on the demonizing rhetoric that vilifies one side or the other. In fact, determining which side is considered good and which is considered bad is a challenge.

It's difficult to imagine a savage culture generating or preserving this epic tale. The description of their society as savage seems incomplete. As C. F. Cusack notes, "Civilization is a relatively arbitrary term; and the ancestors whom we are pleased to term uncivilized, may have possessed as high a degree of mental culture as ourselves, though it unquestionably differed in kind."[16] Certainly when reading Irish myths what seems clear is that they had a distinct and well-defined culture.

Celts were tribal, but not nomads. Ireland was divided up into about one hundred kingdoms and each kingdom was occupied by a tribe or *tuath*. They settled in villages and generally kept a long tenure on their land. This helped them develop a stable culture.

Furthering the notion that the Celts were not simple savages is the fact that they had a well-organized native system of law, known as the Brehon law. These were the oldest surviving laws in Europe[17] with roots not in Roman law but in ancient Indo-European custom. Like many aspects of Celtic society, these laws were not written down. Rather they were passed on orally from one generation to the next. It was not until after Patrick's time—in the seventh century AD—that the Brehon laws were recorded. Brehon law was likely first administered by the druids and later administered by the Brehons (or *brithem*) who were the successors to Celtic druids. They acted as arbiters and interpreters of the law and they were tasked with preserving.

The Celts had a kindred structure to their society. Within the tuath, or tribe, the important unit was the family, not the individual,[18] and the Brehon system of laws matched that structure. The laws were not enforced by a governing authority. Rather they were expected practice within the community. The absence of both a court system and a police force suggests that people did some self-policing. This self-policing would occur within the family groups, who were the entity that would ultimately pay the consequence of the crime. Any offense was not limited to one individual aggrieving another. Potentially, the act of one individual might be required to be rectified by the whole kindred, and this could extend up to four generations.[19]

To modern ears, aspects of Brehon law seem quite progressive. It allowed for surety and seizure of property and recognized divorce and equal rights between the genders and also showed concern for the environment. In criminal law, offenses and penalties were defined in great detail. Restitution rather than punishment was prescribed for wrongdoing. Cases of homicide or bodily injury were punishable by means of fines—the exact amount determined by a scale. Capital punishment was not among the range of penalties available to the Brehons.

So the savage Celts, in contradictory fashion, had a developed culture. A further example of this is their concern about their personal appearance. According to an early Greek historian, soap was a Celtic innovation. The Celts in Gaul also were expert road builders, and the common thought of the well-designed Roman road is more correctly thought of as an improvement on well-designed Celtic roads. Celtic society included a great deal of equality between men and women with women playing prominent and dominant roles in many of their myths.

In addition to oral traditions and laws, the Celts also produced intricate artwork like the *gundestrup* cauldron, a large silver bowl discovered preserved in a peat bog in Denmark, which depicts scenes in multiple panels, and the Tara brooch, which is a beautiful and intricately made adornment featuring gold, silver, copper, amber, and glass. They were clearly more than a group of barbarians. The well-known Celtic scholar Nora Chadwick says of them, "They were the fine flower of the Iron Age, the last phase of European material and intellectual development before the Mediterranean world spread northwards over the Continent and linked it to the world of today."[20] However you define civilization or choose to separate it from savage cultures, evidence from Celtic culture suggests that the assessment of savagery should not be made too quickly.

Language

The Celts did not choose to devote their language to writing. Instead they emphasized oral communication, which gave their culture a relational emphasis and also placed importance on the power of the spoken word. Without written words, all knowledge was regarded as a spiritual possession. There were benefits to their focus on oral communication in terms of increasing memory and oratory skills, but for all the benefits of a verbal communication, the lack of written records was an impediment.

Religion

We could describe the Celts as cultured savages, but they were also known as a religious people. J. A. MacCulloch writes, "Things of the spirit have never appealed in vain to the Celtic soul and long ago classical observers were struck with their religiosity."[21] The Celts' religion was as important as their common language in binding together the numerous tribes that spanned the continent. They ascribed a mystical sense of spirituality to everything around them. To the Celts, the world was alive, and even today the spiritual aspect of the Irish terrain is palpable. The physical world, including the animals, had direct connections to the people. Irish nature was so alive as to have the possibility of enmeshing itself with human life. "They believed that gods, druids, poets and others in touch with the magical world could be literal shape shifters."[22] They could be a person one moment and transform into an animal the next. A poem accredited to Ameairgen, the first druid of Ireland, reads:

> I have been a blue salmon
> I have been a wild dog
> I have been a cautious stag…
> …I have been dead, I have been alive
> I am a composer of songs
> For I am Taliesin.[23]

In keeping with their shape-shifting beliefs, the Celts after Patrick tell an epic tale of one of their ancestors who did not board the ark, but nevertheless survived the great deluge by turning into a salmon. They were not surprised by a shape-shifter; likewise they not surprised when other worldy or supernatural beings found expression in their lives. Their epic tales are full of the appearance of fairies and of people becoming superhuman. Their own heroes often took on superhuman characteristics. To them, the barriers between physical beings and spirits was thin.

Celts have been described as dreamers, and much that is spiritual and romantic in European literature is due to their influence. Scholars note that

> a beautiful dignity hangs over the Irish mythology, an orderliness, a sense of fitness. All the gods are beautifully dressed and most are of startlingly beautiful appearance. It is only by contrast with other mythologies that we realize that the "'land of promise'" contains little that is ugly. There is no sin and punishment…The heathen Irish erected a spirituality—a spiritual loveliness which comes close to an ideal spiritual existence.[24]

Ancient songs describing this land of promise contain some of the loveliest imagery in Irish mythological tradition. This land is sometimes physical and sometimes supernatural. "It is a land where there is naught but truth; without death or decay, or sadness, or envy, or jealousy, or hate, or gloom, or pride, a land of plenty, of flocks and herds, of the ever young, of flowers and fruit."[25]

This creation of an ideal spiritual world runs parallel with an almost flippant attitude about the physical world. They didn't feel the need to create towns to promote commerce or increase security. Instead, invading Vikings created and established towns for them. Even in Christian Ireland the largest centers of gathering were monasteries. They did not unify their tuaths, even for strategic reasons, which made them easy targets for outside enemies. They did not establish a currency until Norse invaders created it for them. The Irish, in many senses, were dreamers, focusing their energies on what was transcendent rather than what was material.

Druids

Gaius Julius Caesar (100–44 BC) describes three classes of Celtic people in Gaul, the intellectuals called druids (*Druides*), the military caste (*Equites*), and the people (*Plebs*). In particular, in later Celtic cultures, druids occupied an important role in society. They were the mystics, the seers, the brain trust. They had influence in many areas of daily life. Celts placed themselves under the authority of their spiritual seers and prophets, the druids. The druids explained the spiritual world as it interacted with the tangible world. They also acted as intermediaries between the people and their spirits and gods.

The druids set prohibitions. Caesar notes, "The Druids believe that their religion forbids them to commit their teachings to writing…because they did not want their doctrine to become public property, and in order to prevent their pupils from relying on the written word and neglecting to train memories."[26] It seems—to scholars such as Peter Berresford Ellis and others—that the Celts, with their well-defined and intricate culture, chose illiteracy rather than being trapped in it. The druids defined this prohibition, and their rationale for prohibiting writing may seem odd to modern ears, but it is in step with romantic, purist, and superstitious Celtic tendencies. It also seems the best explanation for the contradiction between the advanced nature of the Celtic society and its lack of written records. It also partly explains later enthusiasm of the Irish for scholarly pursuits.

Inasmuch as Celtic religiosity was transcendent, otherworldly, and appealing it also had its dark side. The shape-shifting spirits that were very real in the Celtic worldview were not necessarily friendly. Morrigan, a vexingly beautiful otherworldly character in *The Tain*, presents herself to Cú Chullain prior to one of his battles and opposes him by saying, "I shall go in the form of an eel under your feet in the ford so that you shall fall." And "I shall drive the cattle over the ford to you while I am in the form of a grey she-wolf."[27] To the Irish "traps seem to lie hidden at every crossroads and trickster gods lurk behind every tree."[28]

It was a world full of land mines. Inanimate objects could possess the power of reason and will. This was often disconcerting, particularly when you were under a curse. We think of the watchful eye of big brother as a modern difficulty, however to the Irish any animal could be a spy or their enemy. As Thomas Cahill says, "however wonderful this instability may have seemed to the conscious Irish imagination, it had its dark side as well, for it suggested subconsciously that reality had no predictable pattern, but was arbitrary and insubstantial. There is within this world view a terrifying personal implication: that I myself have no fixed identity but am like the rest of reality, essentially fluid, essentially inessential."[29]

The druids, who held significant power over the people, were the ones with the knowledge to make sense of this shifting, unseen realm. They were the ruling class, who gained their power by knowledge gained through mystical divination and "oak knowledge." Learned people in many ancient cultures linked knowledge and religious insight to oak trees, presumably because the oak was a significant and long-lasting tree.

The druids also had the power to use and define words. They not only preserved the relatively stable Brehon laws, but they also established the various taboos, or geis, that the Irish lived under. Theirs was the power to pronounce a geis over anyone and that geis would henceforth influence the fate of that person. Geis were not pronounced lightly, but when they were, they could trump any earlier code or precedent. The power of a geis was above human and divine jurisdiction and brushed aside all previous rulings establishing a new order through the wishes of the person controlling it.[30]

The geis not only exemplifies the scope of druidic power but also the fluidity within the culture. It was a critical part of Irish life, leaving them prisoners of fate and out of control of their own destiny. The Irish heroes of mythic tales seem to care little about breaking taboos, as would be expected of someone larger than life, but in the end, the curses come to rest on them with devastating results. In fact, Cú Chulain, the youthful warrior hero glorified in *The Tain*, ends up dying when being confronted with a double-bind taboo in which no course of action he takes will free him. The geis therefore is seen as inescapable for all. For if the Hound of Culain cannot escape it, then no one can.

Druids held sway over the people in other ways. The druids, who seem to have been drawn to spiritual purity, turned that longing for purity into a curse. They believed that truth was a kind of supreme power. When a king spoke truth and ruled well, the land produced rich crops. When he spoke falsely, the grass refused to grow. Truth was sacred and divine and not to be profaned. It is a wonderful concept in a way, but the result of this desire for purity was a restrictive bondage that placed people under the power of capricious words and deprived them of written language.

The Total Celtic Picture

The culture of Ireland in the fifth century was a blend of order, sophistication, longing for perfection, superstition, and savagery. It sounds in some ways like our world: difficult to describe, complex, and full of double binds that often make life unbearable. There is plenty of opportunity for positive change in their culture, but also much in the culture that is good, wrapped almost inextricably around the destructive parts. We want to do more than just to paint a multifaceted picture of Irish culture; we want to find the Irish core—the thing about their culture that was deeply troubled and thus made the Celts uniquely receptive to transformation.

What Made the Celts Receptive?

What makes a people group convert en masse? Irish culture presented many evidences of misdirection and pain. Before Christianity, few Irish monarchs died a natural death. Most were murdered or assassinated. But often there's a dissatisfaction with the old ways of doing things that somehow culminates in a significant break with the past that leaves a societal void. In Hawaii, there is a story of King Liho Liho, who broke a significant and longstanding taboo by eating food in public from a table prepared only for women. Finding himself surprisingly alive after that audacious act of defiance, he also had the bravery and authority to declare that, from that point onward, taboos would no longer have any significance on the islands. In essence, he declared that the people's former religion was void. Six months later, in what seems too coincidental to not be providential, the first Christian missionaries arrived on the islands. The Hawaiians, having created their own sense of need and finding themselves in a rare state of spiritual void, converted en masse.

Shrinking Irish Territory

There may have been similar providence in pre-Christian Ireland. There certainly was concern amongst the Irish Celts over their shrinking territory and recognition that their isolated days were numbered. There may have been fear that interaction with the outside, meaning Rome, was inevitable. The druids communicated with each other, and those in Ireland would've been aware of the changes happening on the continent. Guerilla raids made by the Irish on Roman settlements indicated that the Irish were not passive in their isolation. Savage they had been, but unaware they were not. They were a culture in some uncertainty and isolation.

The gospel was doubtless communicated by relating it to needs of the culture. We know the Galatians (who were Celts) were vulnerable to enslavement and particularly affected by the message of freedom as presented by Paul to them. Perhaps the Irish Celts, who clearly saw the spiritual ideal that was possible, also longed for that same kind of freedom from their culturally enslaving ways.

Most likely the gospel was spoken to ancient Ireland through *The Tain*, the country's epic myth. In fact, I believe this primary Irish epic myth contains a story that highlights the core nature of the Irish predicament—the one that set them up for transformation.

Mastered By Fate

As noted earlier, *The Tain* relates the story of the heroic and youthful warrior Cú Chulainn. Cú is like the Hulk or a transformer who undergoes distortions of his features before battles. He's truly the Irish superhero, and after he has thus been distorted and enlarged, he springs into his scythed chariot, terrifies and then attacks his foes.

If you read about *The Tain* in any other book you will probably read the excerpted description of Cú's distortion. It's commonly recounted, yet it's not the climax or even the most significant element of *The Tain*. The most powerful element of the story is the description of Cú being trapped in a double bind in which he either has to break his word or battle his childhood friend, Fer Diad. Cú makes an oath to the queenly Medb to cease the nightly raids on her troops, and instead Cú agrees to fight any single warrior she chooses to present to him. Cú and Fer grew up with the same foster mother, and were close friends and remain highly skilled in battle. Neither wishes to fight the other, but in one of the darkly humorous passages in *The Tain,* Medb attempts to coax Fer Diad into fighting his foster brother by sending Druids and satirists to recite satires and lampoons against him and otherwise humiliate him with shame, blemish, and disgrace until he changes his mind. Knowing how the Irish were skilled in verbal arts, we can only imagine the extent to which the satirists go to achieve their objective. Fer Diad finally succumbs to their verbal torment as "he deemed it better to fall by shafts of valour and prowess and bravery than by the shafts of satire and reviling and reproach."[31] Thus coaxed into face-to-face combat,

Cú and Fer Diad find various ways to numb their feelings as they battle each other to the death.

The story presents the heart of angst in the Irish society—the pain that kept them from realizing their spiritual and transcendent ideals. Fer Diad is every bit Cú's equal with the exception that Cú can wield the terrifying and mysterious weapon "ga bulga." After three days of fighting—at the end of each they commiserate and wish each other well—Cú uses the dreaded ga bulga to slay Fer Diad. Cú utters some words in verse afterward identifying how his heart has changed toward combat in general and also that recount how valiant, famous, and brave Fer Diad was. "There has not come into the centre of battle, nor has Banba ever nurtured, nor has there travelled over land or sea any king's son more famous than Fer Diad."[32] The two heroes, neither of which the story identifies as good or evil, are forced to attack each other and fight to the death because of external forces they can't surmount. They are deeply conflicted and forced down paths they don't want to go because of societal conventions.

The death of Fer Diad is an epic tragedy and somehow encapsulates the Irish sense of being mastered by fate in the end. It speaks of a hopelessness to life that, if ever faced directly, will bring insurmountable pain. It is different from tragedies in other cultures. It's not like Brutus slaying Caesar as there's no political intrigue that motivates either Cú or Fer Diad, but rather it's more equivalent to the despair that would be felt if the Hebrew hero David was forced to battle his beloved friend Jonathan to the death.

Control of the Druids

At a deep level, the epic Irish myth points to the Celts' need for freedom. It highlights their hope (beyond hope) for something that would free them from fate and unlock the control of the druids, who prevented them from realizing their potential due to restrictions and taboos. The Irish were purists who had a romantic and passionate connection to life but, like many romantics, were confounded in their pursuit of pure truth. In the case of the Irish, the confounding force was that of legalism and superstition. They were longing for release from these restrictions.

They were also longing for definition of boundaries. The Irish were familiar with things new. The thought of something new—like Cú's distorted features—was entirely welcome to the Irish. Yet the newness the Celts welcomed every day created a huge mental and spiritual territory, and that territory was too big to navigate. Shape-shifters were the bane of Irish existence inasmuch as they stole a sense of stability. The Irish dealt with a perpetual newness that was like a curse.

The Irish found themselves in a number of restrictive situations that made life burdensome and made them particularly vulnerable to the truth of the gospel.

In their predicament, they were oriented toward accepting new and positive features of the gospel. They were open to the concept of newness. To them the concept of God changing his mind was natural. What they really wanted was not just something new, but substantial newness—newness with a form, newness with boundaries, newness with a direction, newness with a skeleton. They would get all that substance and more.

What has been will be again, what has been done will be done again; there is nothing new under the sun.
—Solomon

In the same way, after the supper he took the cup, saying, "This cup is the new covenant in my blood."
—Jesus of Nazareth

CHAPTER 3

NEWNESS WITH A SKELETON

TO CONSIDER THE effect of the gospel on the Irish, we started by taking an unbiased look at the Irish culture. Now let's take an unbiased look at the gospel. It's a challenge to review something that, for many, has become so familiar, so often talked about, and so painted with clichés. What is the gospel, really? Let's start with the context.

The background to the gospel is painted with the history of another ancient group of people, the Hebrews. Like the Irish, they had heroes and epic tales. Unlike the Irish, the Hebrews recorded their epic tales in writing. That writing has survived generations and includes the Torah (the Law) and the prophets and, when compiled with the story of Jesus and his followers, is called the Bible—the holy book that Patrick would have used to communicate the good news of God—the gospel—to the Irish.

The Bible also contains the words of spiritual leaders and prophets of their day, and we will take it as understood that it contains embedded truth that is significant for people other than Hebrews. Many call it the Word of God to humanity in general.

We'll focus on a peculiar, but important, facet of the book that is relevant to the gospel message.

The Blank Page

About three quarters of the way through the Bible there is a singular and peculiar page. It's totally blank. That blankness is like a simple divider between subjects in a frayed school notebook or an ominous dividing line between the ages. Its emptiness has the power to attract emotions and feelings. It rests clean and unspoiled like that vacuous space that mesmerized you before you began an essay, or article, or testimony. It's the proverbial blank piece of paper facing an author, challenging him to start his novel—the novel that could lead in any direction, especially before the first word is penned. The blankness communicates not only challenge, but also a daunting sense of the unknown. It's full of the hope of creating something new and the fear of making mistakes and revealing yourself. It invites the author to write, or not to write. It imposes few restrictions, except those an author might bring from his own mind and heart.

But this particular blank page exists not in a worn notebook or in a discarded journal, but in a revered and inspired religious book. Its placement stands as a unique symbol of Christianity. No other religion has such a blank page in its document. No other religion portrays a God who places a pause in his book, and from that point changes his mind and his manner of dealing with humanity. No other religion dares to represent the posture of change for God, because that posture carries with it some potentially unappealing characteristics. If God pauses to change his mind, maybe he did not know what he was doing the first time around. Or, maybe God is just making things up as he goes along. If, perhaps, God's plan pauses and starts over, what does that say about God's eternal planning ability? These are volatile questions, so the thought of an eternal God announcing a completely new chapter in history—complete with a dividing page in his holy book to represent the break—is rare and is, in fact, unique to Christianity.

Nothing comes close to matching it. We could consider the Book of Mormon, for example, as perhaps presenting a further new thought from the heart of God. Imagine that the Book of Mormon continued the pattern that Christians started—of creating something new and breaking off from the parent religion. On closer inspection, that imagination collapses because the Book of Mormon does not claim to declare something new, but rather claims to present "Another Testament of Jesus Christ." There's no clean break as represented by the blank page between testaments and no indication of the turning over of a new leaf in God's economy. Rather, the Book of Mormon claims itself "comparable to the Bible" and sets out with the task of describing a part of Jesus' work, namely how Jesus allegedly revealed himself to the North American native peoples. However you classify the Book of Mormon, it's not something new in the same way the new covenant follows the blank page in the Bible.

The Koran, another holy book, recognizes Jesus, Abraham, Ishmael, Isaac, and Jacob, and the prophets, but it presents a different perspective on their lives than the Bible does—one that distances itself from the newness associated with the blank page. The Koran integrates the prophets into one voice rather than recognizing the inauguration of something new with Jesus. "We make no distinction between any of them" (2:136). Jesus, as the first prophet after the blank page, is not identified as special by the Koran, but as one who proclaims the same message that earlier prophets did.

Further, if you consider the perspective of newness and read through a document like the Koran fully, you again notice its dissimilarity to the Bible because, unlike the Bible, the Koran makes no attempt to represent God as having changed his course or mind in history.

This idea of switching horses or changing gears is unique to Christianity. One might argue it reinforces the validity of the Bible as a true narrative of God's dealings with mankind, because no human author would suggest such a storyline for the Almighty. But this clean slate presents more than an interesting apologetic view. It presents a true turning point. An interesting aspect of this clean slate is how little we discuss it and what that lack of conversation might say about the unexplored treasures we can discover. We have become oddly familiar with the blank page in the Bible and, to suit our view of godliness, we have acted as though it largely was not there.

We will explore the reasons for our choice of ignorance in some detail, but perhaps it largely comes from fearing the unknown. Perhaps we chose ignorance to reinforce our own "sophistication," which we prefer to stepping into unknown territory. Or perhaps we just have a stubborn refusal to adapt. In many ways, the Christian world has adopted a view of the Bible that leans toward integration rather than highlighting the changes. In a way, it's more of an Islamic view of things, exemplified in the verse following:

> Say (O Muslims): We believe in God and that which is revealed unto us and that which was revealed unto Abraham and Ishmael, and Isaac, and Jacob, and the tribes, and that which Moses and Jesus received, and that which the Prophets received from their Lord. We make no distinction between any of them, and unto Him we have surrendered.

We love to integrate the past and find ways to remove distinctions between God's prophets. Perhaps we are drawn to this task in the same way we get drawn toward fixing an old and broken bike. It's a challenging exercise and one that appears necessary. In our case, what appears broken is the fact that God declares himself unchanging, yet we have this troublesome idea of him presenting something "new" to us.

New is a word that easily fuels controversy and, when not doing that, seems to carelessly open doors that lead people off in untested philosophical directions. It is a curious, troublesome, fiery word that seems destined to raise false hopes and then dash them. For all its volatility, *new* is a word that has essentially been archived. Only marketers continue to use it with any determination. Yet despite the volatility associated with the word, "new" hints of coming change, evident throughout the Bible. The first three quarters of the Bible, that Christians call the "Old" Testament (much to the consternation of Jews, who resent the derogatory labeling of their sacred text), is full of indications of God's capacity to change. It's also full of foreshadowing of his anticipated major upcoming change. A few references are worth noting, because God, indeed, does change his mind in terms of how he deals with the people he has made.

This appreciation of God's posture and stance toward us is important and anything but abstract theology. It will fundamentally define whether you will be motivated, joyful, productive, and, most of all, how you will connect with your Creator. From my experience, a solid understanding of the importance of what separates the old from the new protects me from the mind-numbing and soul-destroying theology that regularly gets presented to me from well-meaning preachers and laypeople. In order to fully accept the blank page, we need to distinguish between God remaining constant in his attributes (which he does) and God remaining constant in the way he deals with humanity (which he does not). This is critically important to understand.

God's Plan Changes

The way God deals with people on this planet changes and, one might even say, evolves. He responds to our freedom, he adds to the scope of his covenants, and he participates in the relationship we have with him. Psalm 78 is a good example of the evolving plan in the heart of God as he deals with his people. It describes God's faithfulness in contrast with the people's stubborn unwillingness to obey. In instance after instance, the people are disobedient and God is merciful. After a few iterations of this pattern, God's heart devises a new plan. The final verses of this Psalm graphically portray one of these turning points.

> Then the Lord awoke as from sleep, as a man wakes from the stupor of wine. He beat back his enemies; he put them to everlasting shame. Then he rejected the tents of Joseph, he did not choose the tribe of Ephraim; but he chose the tribe of Judah, Mount Zion, which he loved. He built his sanctuary like the heights, like the earth that he established forever. He chose David his servant and took him from the sheep pens.

God's plan was previously enacted through Joseph's line, but from the time of this psalm forward, David would produce the saving and restoring lineage. It's a point at which God changed his mind. The change is not practically applicable for us today, perhaps; but for those who followed God then, it was significant. Further expectation of redemption from Joseph's lineage was a misguided waste of time. Failing to know and act according to God's current agenda will, at best, make us ineffective, like Steven Covey's well-known example of working with a dull saw. We think taking time to sharpen our saw keeps us from accomplishing things, but taking time to sharpen our focus actually allows us to be more effective.

God changed his mind in the past and foreshadowed that he was going to make a big change in the way he dealt with humanity in the future. In Jeremiah 31, the prophet called it God's new covenant with mankind—his new deal. Jesus called it the good news or gospel. Before we get to that new covenant, it's important to recognize the territory of the old order—its climate and its expectations.

What Came Before

An obvious place to start looking at the territory before the new covenant is the book immediately before the blank page: Malachi. Malachi was a prophet who spoke to the Israelites about one hundred years after they had returned to Palestine. The people of God, the Israelites, had rebuilt their holy city of Jerusalem; they had rebuilt their temple signifying God's returned presence among them and, under Nehemiah, had enjoyed a brief period in which their ancient God-ordained ways were revived. But they had become mechanistic in their practice of following God. They were encouraged by the restoration of their promised land after captivity under the Babylonians, but ultimately, and oddly, it led to spiritual staleness. Malachi, in chapter 2 verse 2, describes a tone of frustration on God's part.

> "If you do not listen, and if you do not set your heart to honor my name," says the LORD Almighty, "I will send a curse upon you, and I will curse your blessings. Yes, I have already cursed them,

because you have not set your heart to honor me. Because of you I will rebuke your descendants; I will spread on your faces the offal from your festival sacrifices, and you will be carried off with it."

Anyone who has read Deuteronomy knows this language—while abrupt, full of emotion, and apparently harsh—is not unique to Malachi or totally foreign to God. Church pulpits sanitize this language, avoid it actually, but many of the chronicles of God's interaction with the Hebrews under the old covenants indicate an intense level of frustration and wrath. And regardless of how carefully it's avoided or how delicately it's interpreted, this wrath is perceived by those of us today who sit in pews and read the Bible. Even in the modern church, it's in the air, communicated between the sentences and in the body language. The unique frustration of God found in Malachi is not just God's passion against sin; it's that his passion has been felt before and things aren't changing. God's desire for justice is constant, but in Malachi he seems like a parent with a stubborn teen, or a marriage partner for whom the latest argument is not just about the facts: it's about all the debris and strife they have allowed to wash through their lives in the past. It's become a toxic stalemate. The Hebrews seem unable to change their lives, and God seems unwilling to adapt to their sin.

It's a dark time and Malachi would be the last book from any Hebrew prophet for four hundred dry and silent years. At the end of the book of Malachi, before God signs off the airwaves for a few centuries, a few verses are left that reside in my Bible under the inserted (and incorrect) topical heading, "The Nature of God's Judgment." A new-covenant topical heading would be "Hope for Restored Relationship" because the verses speak of the hope of things to come and include

- Healing;
- Skipping about like calves released from the stall;
- Restoring the hearts of fathers to their children;
- Restoring the hearts of children to their fathers.

Malachi, it seems, recognizes the severity of the situation and longs, in a prophetic way, for a time when the stubborn teenager and the father will be restored to relationship because he seems to know it can't go on. Teenage rebellion always seems to incite parental wrath, especially at the point when it evidences lack of respect. God feels dishonored (1:6; 1:11) and is angry. All the patches have been applied, all the fixes have been tried, and all that's left apparently is frustration and anger, because what is being suffocated is that which God deems most precious—life.

In this context, Malachi prophesies about what will propel the next era, the new covenant. He scolds the Israelites for their lack of performance in tithing and then, paradoxically, goes on to prophesy that the new covenant will not be driven by performance, but by a desire to restore relationship. The new covenant will be a matter of the heart. And there will be benefits. Fathers will turn their hearts toward children and children will turn theirs toward fathers. The Father of all will initiate this and somehow, after four hundred years of pondering, find a way to direct his heart in an undistracted manner toward his children. The children will, in turn, direct their hearts to the Father. The result will be uncontainable joy and healing.

Could this occur? Given the previous language of Malachi, this change in attitude will take a miracle. Four-hundred years hardly seems long enough to imagine the transformation in heaven and on earth to make this change possible. Whatever miracle does occur will become the fundamental feature of the age to come—the age in which we live. Ignoring the truth of our age will be the ultimate act of wastefulness—the burying of the precious talent. It will be the ultimate act of denial. Likewise, bathing ourselves in the frequency of that change will become the noblest, most enlivening, and most effective of pursuits.

One of the most important and controversial features of Jesus' work is that it will not be something that happens along the continuum. It will, rather, disrupt. It will be a discontinuity. It will eradicate the old and will be something new—and will make everything new. Perhaps that doesn't sound controversial, but it is.

New is not a word to be used lightly in religious or philosophical circles. Yet *new* is a word consistently and repeatedly used by Jesus. Newness is so important to Jesus that he mentions it specifically at the most critical juncture of his life.[1] He uses it purposefully as if recognizing its implications.

If what Jesus brought truly is new, then we are encountering something we have not dealt with before, and we really don't know how to address it or how it should be handled, named, or characterized. A process of discovery will be required, and the person (Jesus) introducing the new thing must recognize that. If he has awareness of the new nature of his product, he will purposefully not use too many words to define it, because the words he uses will, of necessity, be old words and what will result in people's minds from those old words will be an assemblage of old perceptions.

It seems clear. To follow Jesus is to accept the newness he brought. Yet we are pathologically nervous about new things. Acting on a belief that God's doing a new thing feels a bit like jumping off of a cliff. There are enough arguments assembled against that seemingly foolish act to prevent anyone from attempting it for any reason—except a sense of desperation. Desperation is not necessarily bad, but let's also give ourselves some breathing room by reinforcing our minds to stand against the arguments that oppose newness.

The best argument raised against newness is that it doesn't exist. This reasoning responds to apparent newness with the statement, "Nothing is truly new." This wall defends us against claims of newness because new products always seem to reveal themselves as nothing more than the recycled products of old material. Philosopher Henri-Charles Puech goes so far as to say, "No event is unique, nothing is enacted but once...; every event has been enacted, is enacted, and will be enacted perpetually; the same, individuals have appeared, appear, and will appear at every turn of the circle."[2] He articulates the final voice of cynicism, the final chokehold on discovery. In some sense, it's a curse that in its wording also announces the fear that motivates its pronouncement. Many people know at a deep level that the pursuit of newness treads near to a sort of circular futility. Newness, says Robert Pirsig, is an interesting and enlightening pursuit, but pursued exclusively it results only in "an endless parade of trivia and fashion, the silt of tomorrow."[3] No one wants that kind of life, but denying newness may not be the best way to escape it.

Another argument is that proof of newness is difficult to generate. In scientific terms, we know that mass always gets conserved, as does energy. According to those laws, nothing at an atomic level is ever created. Rather, atoms are just rearranged. But we know that in spite of conservation of mass we are still discovering "new" subatomic particles. They are new to us, so they provide a hint of newness.

In the face of arguments such as those above, we stand with Jesus and his statement that he truly brought something new. We also take some comfort in the knowledge that misguided pursuits that end badly don't negate the value of the true pursuit. And we know that interpretation of any data can be clouded by mistaken perspectives.

So let's start with a fresh perspective—that newness is possible—and begin by looking for some simple examples. We know, for example, that our skin regenerates every month; we know that we get tired of watching and listening to television reruns and old songs. We experience newness on many physical and sensory levels. Babies come into the world the same way babies always have. Yet every baby is unique and every baby has a new fingerprint. Each birth brings something slightly (and perhaps truly) new into the world. Perhaps babies represent the strongest evidence of newness we can point to. They indicate we're not crazy in our acceptance of newness. They build our faith to consider, at the request of Jesus, the possibility of the most ethereal newness—spiritual newness (as if physical newness did not hold enough of the subjective and unquantifiable within it.)

And in choosing to believe in newness, we also start to recognize that in our so-called safe position of denying newness we've often chosen to pave old roads instead of taking new paths. We have preferred to wallow in what often seems like obligatory structures geared toward producing immature and juvenile responses. The sum of those responses leads to lifeless, dull communities. We've integrated with the old (even though it's decaying) when we could've explored the new. We've tried to make sense of the unexplainable uniqueness of what comes after the blank page without first getting baptized in the reality of the blank page. All because we ignore the primary fact that God really wanted to start over again.

The blank page serves as a starting point. More than that, it signifies God's desire to purge old restrictions and turn over a new leaf that can't really be explained. It needs to be discovered: an absolutely terrifying thought to those of us who are not Irish.

Bartender, please
Fill my glass for me
With the wine you gave Jesus that set him free
After three days in the ground
— Lyrics, Dave Matthews

CHAPTER 4

FEATURES OF THE NEW

WE KNOW FROM Malachi, the last of the old prophets, that the Hebrews' relationship with God had deteriorated into what seemed like a bad marriage. It definitely was in need of a fresh start. The four-hundred year period of silence that followed Malachi's prophecy was like a marital annulment. Something new was necessary for the Hebrews and likely for us as well.

Many of us are like the recently divorced when it comes to spirituality. We feel like we've tried to make things work, but we don't know what's solid. We bump into walls. We fall down. We end up in the same old patterns. Spirituality seems like it's for other people. To try to make more sense of it all we turn to religion. Often that produces more questions than it answers. Religion doesn't seem like a safe way to explore spirituality, it often seems more like playing with fire. Some light does pierce through occasionally. God breaks through, touches us, surprises us for a season, and becomes an undeniable and tangible force in our experience. The next day, or month, rules take over. In the end, we drift away and think church isn't for us, chalking everything up to irreconcilable (or unexplainable) differences.

For the Hebrews, beyond the silence, the question remained: "What would God do differently the second time around?" We know God isn't prone to sulking or blaming, he's prone to action.

Considering what we discovered in the last chapter about how babies point to newness, it's not surprising that God's plan for newness begins with a baby—a child who Isaiah tells us in advance will govern and be called wonderful. We mentioned earlier that when pondering the possibility of newness, the most striking example is the miracle of birth. If anything is new in our world it's a new child. Granted, babies come into the world the same way human babies always have. They are born today the same way they were born in centuries past. The process of birth repeats itself thousands of times a day. Yet every baby born has unique DNA. Emphasizing newness from the start, the new covenant is ushered in beginning with a birth. It's the birth of something new.

Heart Laws

We also saw earlier in Malachi that one of God's primary motives was to guarantee a heart connection with his people. The biblical author Jeremiah foretells the new covenant and describes its features (Jer. 31:31–34). We'll look at that significant passage in some detail, but first, we'll note that the passage also includes language of the heart. God says in graphic terms that he'll write his laws on our hearts. He will scribe his words on the core of our being. He will skip intermediate communication and move straight to heart-level interaction. In fact, that goal of heart-level connection becomes the cornerstone of everything that's new. The things that are new will focus on the heart. They will focus on the seat of our being and on our inner lives. The law, if it exists at all, will relate to our hearts.

The ability of any law, even God's law, to manage or supervise matters of the heart is questionable. Can a legal structure facilitate heart relationship? It's hard to imagine, but before we discard it as impossible, we have to look at the kinds of laws that God writes—the kinds of deals he crafts with humanity. We need to take a brief historical look at the concept of covenant. Throughout history, as recorded in the Bible, God made covenants with humanity. They were first spoken and later recorded. They were enacted in a format similar to what was the familiar treaty language of the people.

Sometimes the parties of the covenant walked between the cut parts of an animal to signify ratification. The animal's death signified what would happen to the covenant breaker. In our day, a covenant would look like a legal document with a spot for signatures and possibly seals at the end. We would know by glancing at it that it was important and would likely review it carefully before signing. Afterwards, the document would be posted or filed so it could be reviewed. Like a contract it would become the basis for all further discussion and relationship between the signing parties. It could not, and would not, be revoked except under the severest circumstance such as bankruptcy, death, or dissolution of one party. A covenant, like a contract, defined the terms of relationship—in the case of a biblical covenant, the relationship between God and man.

Why covenants are necessary is another matter. The important thing to note is that they are the tool that God uses to define relationship between him and us. Many of them are one-sided, in that God has all the obligations and maybe even signs for both parties, but that should not deceive us into thinking they are non-important for us. In some ways, the entire Bible is about covenants and each verse either describes a covenant or provides commentary on how the parties are performing in relation to them. To not understand covenants is to not understand the God of the Bible. Covenants are the words of God to his people and just as the world functions according to the physical laws, the world we now live in functions according to his relational or covenantal laws.

Covenants in the past included those given to Adam, Noah, Abraham, David, and Solomon. The covenant we now live under is called the new covenant. The new covenant, in what may seem contradictory language, is a binding formal contract with a heart connection as a driving force. It's a love law, a heart code, a relational rule book. God created the code so that, like the laws of the Medes and Persians, it can't be broken. In what is a major departure from previous practice, God chooses to record the law organically—on our hearts. This sounds almost like a sci-fi movie, yet it is real. Our hearts are the paper on which God communicates. His rules are inscribed on our inner beings. Our minds and emotions serve as a scroll for God. This is a significantly new concept.

No Specific Words

Luke, in his gospel account, describes Jesus as he ushers in the new covenant: "he took the cup, saying, 'This cup is the new covenant in my blood, which is poured out for you...'"

A simple and succinct statement loaded with significance. As he held the cup, Jesus equated himself and his blood directly with the new covenant. They are made to seem one and the same. This is odd, but not totally without precedent in covenantal language. The covenant is exclusively described with objects, people, and symbols. While it's consistent with Jeremiah's prophecy, it's also extremely unique. If Luke's kids were in a memory course and had just completed memorizing all of God's previous covenants, they'd have difficulty getting their final star for memorizing the new covenant because there are really no words to memorize.

Jesus chose his culminating moment to explain his purpose. On the eve of his death, he took part in a ritual that would usher in the new covenant. He used words that would leave no doubt. In an upper room, eating a Passover meal with his twelve closest followers, he made the proclamation. He knew the cross in all its agony would occur the next day. After that, it would all be newness. The cross would complete the last of the fulfillments of the old covenants. Jesus' delivery of the new covenant is powerfully symbolic and important. He purposely omits words to define it. There are no words to treasure, no words to categorize, and no words to deify. The basis of the covenant is a person, the cup he is about to drink, and the words that will come out of the covenant will be written on our hearts.

Gone are the days in which the emphasis is on the recorded words, gone is the ability to abuse the written words of God by focusing on words rather than the author. The new covenant creates an end to the significance and the religious power of the written or memorized word. It does so not by debasing the written word, but by providing something superior.

In covenant perspective, the implications are significant. The terms of the deal are not written in words. The deal rather consists of, is held by, and mediated entirely by a person. The deal purposely is not governed by written words and thus has a relational, unbounded, and partly mysterious nature. Since the words of it are written on our hearts, the deal can never ultimately be completely defined to us by others, nor can the terms of the deal be used as a weapon against us. The covenant may benefit from written words, but it is not dependant on them or on any book. Words that are significant in our age are those that describe the outworking of the deal and will be of an unbounded nature. They will continue to be written and are continually written as we relate with God and explore his nature.

This is mind-blowingly significant and is rarely discussed, even two thousand years later. Why? Because we protect our written words very carefully. They provide our precedents, our links to the old, our security, our safety from foolishness. My Mennonite ancestors once made a film to describe their history and titled it *People of the Book*. Not a bad title, but not a new-covenant one. They didn't call it *People of the Word*, or *People of Jesus*. They focused on adherence to, and reverence for, a book. The title misses a more important Christian point. *People of the Book* could be a movie about Hindus or Muslims, as well as Christians. Most religions have a book to describe and define their faith. Every faith wants to record and plant "correct and pure" words of life in people's minds. The Bhagavad Gita, the Koran, and the Bible show that people recognize the power of written words and also have the need to protect words that bring life from being defiled by death-producing words. Only Christianity breaks from that pattern and places the book in our hearts and says there really is only one Word and it's a person. It's an astoundingly unique and risky feature of our faith.

But it's a feature that often gets clouded because of familiarity or through misconception associated with old baggage. We need to find a way to let the biblical description of the gospel become new in our minds. His covenant today is new. We need to get back some of that perspective. Paul had to spend years in the desert contemplating the staggering realities of what was new and how it might affect his rational, trained, Hebrew mind. The early church was in fact quite slow to adopt some features of the new covenant. For example, early Christians believed that you were forgiven of your past sins, but you only stayed saved until your next sin. It's one of the early theological questions Paul likely wrestled with in the desert. With centuries of the church's theological wrestling behind us, we can see this perspective was a holdover from the old covenant. It's like a father saying to the teen, "If you screw up one more time, you'll be out of here so fast." Why would God adopt a posture of remembering sin when that proved to suffocate relationships before? What he wanted was a relationship with us that can't be blocked by any barrier.

Not Dependent on Perfect Theology

We'll explore more features of the new covenant ahead, but an important starting point to remember is that the new covenant experience is mysterious, experiential, adventuresome, and not dependent on perfect theology. In fact, the new covenant confirms that we are always growing in our knowledge of God. We may know more than the early church did. We know how to craft statements of faith, but we don't know everything. As we get older, we grow in knowledge. One truth starts the process and others get added. In between the two it can be fuzzy. It is a dialectical process. The relationship is the web that connects one place of understanding to the next. The house of wisdom gets enlarged one beam, one post at a time. Since we don't know everything and since the new covenant is not dependent on theology, our troubling concerns about God can be effectively shelved. Any conundrum that restricts or dampens the growth of the faith in our hearts is a problem that can be temporarily placed aside because God is operating from a new perspective that places the heart at a level above all else. He wants to risk everything to get your heart. It doesn't mean that thinking or understanding isn't important. It just means that all our understanding of God needs to grow out of a perspective of heart relationship. Otherwise it's likely faulty.

Verses often used to come to my mind that seemed to conflict with the new-covenant perspective. But I realized that a new perspective does not wash over old theology in an instant. If there's one thing that we can learn through studying the life of Jesus and his interaction with scholars of his day, it is how easily we become led away from life-giving truth. It is also a curiously human tendency to develop and defend mental and theological constructs that keep us in the lies we have been led into. We need to let truth transform our thinking over time. In the meantime, build on the solid blocks—the ones that have made a difference in your own life—and shelve the theological blocks that don't fit (for a while). Chances are they don't fit because your old theology has misinterpreted them as round when in fact they are square.

An important thing to remember is that even though the rules have changed, solidity still exists. In Psalm 25:10 David says, "All the ways of the LORD are loving and faithful for those who keep the demands of his covenant." In Genesis 17:9 God said to Abraham, "As for you, you must keep my covenant, you and your descendants after you for the generations to come."

If you like constancy, then you can take comfort in the fact that we're still bound to God by covenants. We just have to be aware of the covenant we're under now—and it's focused on relationship, not law.

The church, despite its reluctance to embrace the new covenant, has inexorably moved toward making decisions in the new-covenant direction. The church has slowly but relentlessly become less code focused and more governed by relational reality. Likewise, the world, since Jesus, has become a more new-covenant place. If relationship with our Creator is paramount, then people must be important; individuals must have value and authority. Those who receive revelation gain authority. When God spoke to Pharaoh through Joseph, Pharaoh recognized the authority in Joseph and made him his second in charge. In the desert, God spoke exclusively to Moses so the people listened to him. Biblical prophets and pagan shamans have the ability to rebuke kings and live. Thus they hold a privileged position in society. Whoever God speaks to gains authority, and today God speaks to all people—so people have the authority.

The reality that people have authority has fuelled the great individualist movements of our time. In this age we have seen the replacement of monarchical rule, which does not blend well with the new covenant, with various forms of self-government. These all have their own flavor, but all resonate with the same heartbeat—the people want to exercise their authority and govern themselves. Individuals must have a say. The French Revolution, immediately followed by the American Revolution, then the Russian Revolution all had this common thread. It's not only western. India and Japan have democratic governments as well. People power is not limited to any one sphere of the earth.

Jesus planted a seed of truth in the universe. Individuals are more significant than they were before. They have authority. People, in ways both brave and foolish, have acted on this truth and so altered the structures of society to fit it.

Paul firmly latched on to the nature of new covenant and never shied away from acting consistently with it regardless of how radical or dangerous it may have seemed. To the Galatians (Celts) he held out two standards by which they should measure false messages that might detract from the incredible experience that changed their lives: the absolute truth of the gospel (the message he preached) and the individual, internal, experience they had (the message they accepted). He holds both out in equal measure as valid reference points. He does not minimize their experience or their personal revelation; he gives it great value while at the same time holding it accountable to the absolute truth.

Which brings us back to the Irish and Patrick, but first let's summarize the features and implications of the new covenant.

Features and Implications of the New Covenant

- **New:** God has overthrown the old order of things and created a new covenant or deal with humanity. It is not

like the old deal. It supersedes it. This new deal creates the structure of our age.
- **Relational**: God is now reaching out. The reason for terminating the old covenant and the goal of the new was to encourage heart-to-heart connection between God the Father and his children. Jesus' task was relationships. He first assembled twelve men with whom he could develop a real and close relationship, then moved out to minister to the crowds. He related to men, women, children, governors, foreigners, the poor, the crippled, and the educated at a deep level. He was often moved by compassion for people, to the point of tears in the case of Lazarus.
- **Wordless**: The terms of the deal are not written in words. Jesus presented himself as the mediator of the deal and symbolized it with a cup that symbolized his blood. Jesus spoke or wrote no further words to define the deal. The deal is rather defined by symbols representing the one who called himself the Word. The deal consists of, is held by, and mediated entirely by a person. It is purposely not governed by written words and thus has a relational, unbounded, and partly mysterious nature. It can never ultimately be defined or used as a weapon by others as the words of it are on our hearts. It may be benefited by written words, for example the words recorded in the Bible, but it is not dependent on a book. Words that describe the outworking of the deal will be near us, in our mouths and in our hearts as we relate with God.
- **Inclusive**: Peter's first sermon emphasized the new covenant was inclusive. He stressed inclusiveness by quoting the prophet Joel, who said everyone—sons, daughters, young men, old men, women, and servants—would receive God's revelation.
- **Internal**: The deal recognizes the importance of people's inner lives—their hearts and minds. These will be the faculties by which the deal will be communicated. The theme of the new covenant's only rite—Communion—is our inner world. When we eat the bread and drink the cup we graphically

symbolize Jesus working from the inside. Jesus comes and works inside us and changes the world through us.
- **Individual:** The deal focuses on direct relation between God and individuals. That will, at a fundamental level, negate the requirement for one person to teach another.[1] (Perhaps all we really do when we teach is remind each other of the truth.) There will be a subjective component to the deal. All relationships of the new covenant build from the cornerstone of each individual's direct relationship with the Word himself—Jesus. It's an individual corporateness. The Word is Jesus and Jesus does not only broadcast his message. The Word to each heart is unique and personal, and that uniqueness enhances our community.

The following comparison table shows differences between the new and old covenants. This table simplifies all covenants before the new, groups them, and classes them as old.

Old	New
Legal, defined by clauses of law.	Relational, defined by a person, Jesus.
Objective, coded on paper or stone.	Subjective, coded on hearts.
Defined by words, bounded in scope.	Defined by no words, unbounded in scope.
Characterized by performance.	Characterized by adventure and discovery.
Exclusive, applicable to a nation.	Inclusive, applicable to all.
Sin a primary feature, defined as impurity.	Sin a resolved issue, defined as lack of faith, love.
Characterized by indirect communication.	Characterized by direct communication.

The new supersedes the old, but the two eras have similarities in the following ways:

- Obedience to God's initiative remains important in the new,
- Humility remains important in the new,
- Risk taking (faith) remains important in the new.

I've come to believe the best way to connect with God in the world we live in is to connect with the truth he has presented to us. Many of my questions about religion and God have led me to the feature of newness. What God presents to us happens to be something we want as much as he does—a mindset that releases the old and welcomes the new.

Lastly, thinking of spiritual newness often requires consideration with the right part of brain. We must move slightly outside the realm of data and logic. It's not being irrational or illogical. It's just recognizing we're in different territory and we may not have all the assumptions correct. Spirituality is associated with things we cannot fully perceive with our senses and things that appear to operate under different cause-and-effect relationships than we're used to.

Consider, for example, spirituality as wind. In my front yard the wind sways the branches of the weeping willow, and the way it makes the branch tips bend under its force and nick against our bedroom window pane makes me think of God's Spirit. I know wind is real and experience the weather it creates, but the best and brightest forecasters can barely predict its movements a few days in advance. We know it can respond very differently than what we expect—a small action can cause a large reaction. In many ways I see God like the wind, blowing through the city and blowing through and around people's bodies and lives, yet not being visible. Stirring the ocean, bending trees, and rustling leaves: having the power to move turbines and also to make eyelids flutter. Being the air we breathe and our motive force—if we choose to set our sails.

If wind does symbolize God's Spirit (and it is noted as such throughout the Bible), then it's interesting that in the symbol of wind we see the divide between old and new. In the old economy—before the blank page—wind was predominantly, but not entirely, destructive. It scorched deserts, brought locusts, and rained upon the wicked (together with sulfur). It wasn't something you readily let yourself be influenced by or let yourself be swayed under. It was something you resisted or fled from. After the blank page, however, wind is different. Jesus rebukes the wind and it becomes calm, as do the waves it creates. From his rebuke onward, wind becomes not entirely, but predominantly, good. It delivers the Holy Spirit to the disciples in the upper room, albeit violently. Those born of the Spirit are compared to the wind. Angels gather the elect from the four winds. Wind continues to have power like it did before, but now it's a power we can welcome. We can allow ourselves to be swayed by it.

Wind, in our world, still foils plans and destroys docks. It is not contained or controlled. It is still surprising and thus a very good metaphor for the Holy Spirit and God. It just has more of a sense of blessing wrapped around it. In that way it is symbolically transformed.

Keep the new-covenant features in mind as we turn our focus back to the Irish and look at the person who communicated the gospel to them first. Patrick's story is a new-covenant tale.

CHAPTER 5

PATRICK

THE IRISH, AFTER centuries of avoiding Roman influence, received the gospel at the hands of a Roman bishop. In fact, two Roman bishops were commissioned to Ireland in the fifth century: Palladius and Patrick. Palladius, being first in line, was in the best position to leave his legacy with the native people of Ireland. He was ordained as bishop to the Irish by Pope Celestine in 431. One reason he is not as well known as Patrick is that we hear nothing more of him after his commissioning. The information void is so complete—nothing is written of his journey and nothing about any subsequent contact or exploits—that while it's possible he managed to have significant impact on the Irish while also keeping a low profile, it's more likely that he never made it to Ireland at all, or possibly returned shortly after he did.

That leaves Patrick. With a modern persona cloaked in green from head to foot and the mention of his name inseparable from green beer, shamrocks, leprechauns, and four-leaf clovers, the suggestion that Patrick was a pioneering messenger of the new covenant goes against popular perceptions. Uncovering a powerful and influential Patrick seems, at first glance, as likely as unearthing the real Santa Claus. Yet, as it turns out, a modest search reveals a surprising amount of substance behind the man of green, including at least two documents penned by the man himself: *Confession* and *Letter to the Soldiers of Coroticus*. From these we know, for example, that he was not Irish. Patrick was actually a Romanized Celt born in western Britain in the late fourth century (about AD 385). He was not known as Paddy, but by his Roman name, Patricius. He was born the son of a local decurion, or town leader, in a town in the far reaches of the empire.

Like Palladius, he was sent as a bishop to Ireland. Unlike Palladius, Patrick was sent from Gaul, not Rome, and there remain records of his life and his death. Irish annals at the time of his death record Patrick as a cherished son of his adopted country. Exploits of his followers confirm him as one of the world's most outstanding and effective missionaries. He had such far-reaching success at this task that he became a world-changing historical character.

If Patrick is worth studying as the man of missionary exploits, he is also worth considering because of his character and personality. Those not inclined toward history can also connect with him because he conveys simple, honest, and raw emotions and seems devoid of pretense. He left his home to evangelize people for whom few else cared.[1] He was one who spoke plainly and described his faith in the same way he described his daily life: with passion, honesty, and vulnerability.

His Story

As mentioned, Patrick's father was a decurion, or town leader. His grandfather was a presbyter. That lineage confirms Patrick's family had longstanding connections to Rome. Roman connections would have given the family certain privileges, and those are evident in the surroundings of which he writes. His father had a country residence and Patrick had teachers. He was born into the upper class. He referred to himself as being from Banna Venta Berniae, but there is no consensus as to where this is located in Britain. South Wales seems a likely candidate given its Roman history and, for reasons we shall learn, given its proximity to the Irish Sea.

All the significant events of Patrick's lifetime are framed by the common theme of Roman decline and retreat. Fifty years before

Patrick's birth,[2] Constantine moved the capital of the empire to Constantinople, placing distance between the seat of power and the various intruders. Twenty years before Patrick, Picts and Scots attacked Roman garrisons in Britain. About the time that young Patrick was a teenager, groups of barbarians, consisting of Alans, Sueves, and Vandals were invading the Iberian Peninsula and conquering four of the five Roman provinces there. Yet despite the turmoil around him, Patrick lived his early life in the fashion of other young Romans living in Wales at the time—the life of privilege. He was likely an unmotivated youth. In his *Confession*, he documents a teenage malaise and contempt for authority, saying, "We neither kept his [God's] commandments nor obeyed our priests who used to warn us about our salvation." The young Patrick appeared to have few strong ideas about religion, newness, or life, and the ideas that he did have were counter-cultural. He was not, it appears, out to change the world. In fact, he had hardly begun to mature.

With the retreat of the empire came the retreat of ordered civilization, the closing of centers of learning, and increased uncertainty about the future. Roman disintegration also allowed external forces more ability to exercise their influence, and these external forces affected Patrick directly. At the tender and tumultuous age of sixteen, his teenage apathy was shaken to the core. He discovered while traveling (likely daydreaming) to his father's country residence what it was like to endure gut-wrenching change. He was caught up with thousands of others, including his servants, and taken captive in an Irish raid.

These were raids the Irish were renowned for and their goal was to obtain slaves. They would sneak into unsuspecting harbors and head back to sea with their cargo before any resistance could be mustered. The more youthful the slaves, the better, as youth could provide more years of service. At sixteen, Patrick was a prime catch. After being whisked across the Irish Sea, he found himself, by most scholarly estimates, on the west coast of Ireland in County Mayo. In the woods and mountains of that coast, he worked for his new master by tending sheep in inhospitable conditions. He experienced day after day of isolation and he endured nakedness and hunger. He was forced into the elements, into labor, and into the loneliness felt by all strangers in strange lands.

Some men long for newness and others have newness thrust upon them. Patrick was definitely in the latter category. He went from a person of standing, a Roman with rights and hope for the future, to a slave with no standing, rights, or hope. He was dragged into a new life that was drastically different from his upper-class upbringing. Being Welsh, he was a Celt, but he was also a third-generation Roman and, thus, likely not taught any Celtic languages. Initially, he would have not understood his captors. Yet in the midst of his harsh new environs, his loneliness, and his limited freedom, something started to stir and burn within him.

Something about his limited options drove him to discover the faith that he had previously scorned. He says of this time that he awoke early and prayed hundreds of times each day. Given the harsh climate and his lack of shelter, it's no surprise that he didn't sleep late; but when he awakened early, he chose to focus on something other than bitterness and anger. He chose to understand the love of God more and more. For some reason, the hardship of his captivity transformed him from a sullen youth to a man of God. Psalm 119:71 says, "It was good for me to be afflicted so that I might learn your decrees." Patrick's affliction allowed him to meet the God who makes the decrees. In the midst of his affliction, he becomes a different man.

His journey from that point onward literally becomes the stuff of legend. To avoid the embellishment and exaggeration that characterizes many of those legends, our description will focus on the primary documents we have regarding his life—both written by the man himself.

Patrick leaves out details regarding where he was captive. In fact, Patrick leaves out many details. His choice of topics in his *Confession* confirms that he saw the invisible and emphasized that aspect at the expense of almost everything else. In that sense, he was a true Celt. He has a frustrating habit of only discussing topics in the *Confession* that relate to significant encounters with God—almost as if other details are irrelevant. It's a writing style that, while difficult for a historian, matched well with Irish predispositions toward the romantic and the unseen. He doesn't tell us where, or for exactly how long, he was a slave, but he does tell us he spent six years with his last master, so we know he endured slavery for a significant time. We also know that when he left his captors, he was no longer a teen.

Patrick told the story about his departure from slavery by focusing on the encounters with God that preceded and surrounded that event. His first recorded encounter occurred while he was out in the elements, in his sleep.

"It is well that you fast, for soon you will go to your own country," a voice told him. A short time later a voice also said, "Look, your ship is ready."

Patrick exercised his characteristic obedience, heeded God's instruction, and simply left his captors. He walked, without resistance, about two hundred miles to the Irish shore.

"And I went in the strength of God who directed my way to my good, and I feared nothing until I came to that ship."

Joseph Duffy, the bishop of Clogher, and biographer of Patrick, notes that slavery was common throughout the area we now know as western Europe at the time, and the economic structure of society depended on slaves. Members of such a society had little motivation to aid an escaping slave. Yet, Patrick managed to navigate the perilous journey to the shore and, having obviously learned the language, negotiated with a boat captain to take him aboard. The boat headed south and reached land after three days. Then, for twenty-eight days, Patrick and the crew traveled through a deserted country where they ran out of food. The desperate captain taunted Patrick, saying that if he was a Christian and if his God is all-powerful then why didn't he pray for them? Patrick was young, but he knew hunger and he also knew God's power.

"Turn sincerely with your whole heart to the Lord my God, because nothing is impossible for Him, that this day He may send you food on your way until you be satisfied; for He has plenty everywhere," Patrick said.

This response to the captain provided an insight into Patrick's character, which, by the end of his captivity, had become stripped of bitterness. He emerged from an extended period of deprivation with a surprising belief in a God "who has plenty everywhere"! This belief seems completely illogical based on his previous circumstances, but completely true when a herd of pigs suddenly appeared on the road before them, and "they killed many of them and they stopped there for two nights. They were well fed and had their fill of pork for many of them had grown weak and had been left half-dead along the way."[3]

Connecting abundant provision from the land with the goodness of the people who rule over, or otherwise have charge of, the land, is a common concept in pre-Christian Irish records. Irish historical annals often associate the rule of a good king with abundant and excess produce of the land and sea.[4] Patrick's language to the sailors not only revealed his belief in the goodness of God who will provide, but it also revealed how his outlook on life during his captivity became Irish.

The night following the experience of the provision of food, Patrick, who seems as familiar with encounters with God as with spiritual opposition, wrote that he felt a weight so heavy on his chest that he could not resist beneath it. He wrestled against the weight for some time with no success until, at dawn, he called out for Elijah and was subsequently sustained by Christ, as his spirit called out on his behalf. Other passages written by Patrick retain the same sense of the immediacy of spiritual battle. The breastplate of St. Patrick—a prayer that was not part of his *Confession*, but if not written by him, then one surely influenced by his life—is full of references to battle with spiritual foes in daily life.

His desert journey ended after sixty days and he eventually returned to his native Britain, home to his relatives. He did not say what became of his parents in the meantime, but they apparently were no longer there. His relatives welcomed him as a son and, understandably, wished him to never leave again. He stayed with them a few years and, characteristically, did not give details. He had matured and transformed since they last knew him, so perhaps his return was awkward as well as joyful. One night, while at home, he had a vision. Like most of Patrick's encounters with God, he wrote it without much commentary, yet it was profound and worth reflection. In this vision, a man named Victor—who was obviously from Ireland—presented Patrick with a staggering number of letters, which open with the words, "The voice of the Irish." As Patrick began to read the letters he also heard the voices of those by the Western Sea saying together, "We ask you, holy boy, come and walk once more among us."[5] Patrick is cut to the heart at this point and cannot read more. It's the kind of dream that you wake from with a gasp and a feeling of wonder.

This dream constituted Patrick's call to the Irish and was steeped in new-covenant principles. The dream set the groundwork for his mission. It was personal and direct and did not include requests to lead the Irish, change them, or show them the way. The call was devoid of an agenda, except relationship. The call recognized what Patrick had become—holy—and merely asked him to come and walk among them. It was a call to relationship with a hint that from that relationship change would result. It was a call from those who were formerly his captors to return to them. It was striking, radical, and potentially dangerous—the kind of features that played prominently in the call from a God who, in this new covenant, wants most to restore the hearts of the children to the Father.

On another night, Patrick received another message from God confirming that he would be given what it took to meet the Irish need. In this dream, he perceived someone speaking the most learned language he had ever heard, but he could not understand it. All he could understand from the dream were the last words of the message: "He who gave his life for you, he it is who is speaking in you."[6] He awoke full of joy.

Patrick received his call in a way that struck at his sense of compassion and also filled him with joy. While he moved to fulfill his call, he was faced with struggle, but it is worth noting his call was not to surrender, die, fulfill an obligation, or keep people from hell. Rather, his call was to find the place of his own joy as he chose to relate to those who needed him. He was filled with a sense of God empowering him to fill his mouth with the necessary words. This call, most certainly, confirmed Patrick as the mentor of the Irish, because later Irish missionaries who populated the continent after the retreat of Rome had a similar perspective. They did not primarily travel the seas out of obligation. Rather, their going was an expression of one of their loves—the love of wandering—and when they wandered they went "seeking the place of one's resurrection."[7] From the earliest moment of the Irish evangelistic enterprise, we see the emphasis being placed—before the message was uttered—on the intrinsic power and appeal of the message rather than on the obligation of the preacher to preach it or the listener to receive it.

Patrick prepared for his task by attempting to make up for his lack of education. Monasteries were the seat of learning at that time and he received training at a monastery in Gaul. We do not know for how long he was there, but it was likely a period of years, because he talks about close friends in Gaul, and his work in Ireland seemed influenced by the monastic traditions. Regardless of how long his stay was, it was sufficient to enable him to be ordained as a bishop at the end of that period and be sent "to preach the gospel and disseminate religion and piety among the Irish." Without slighting Patrick's abilities—since he was a relative newcomer and by his own admission was "most unlearned"—it would almost appear that competition for the posting of bishop of Ireland was not intense. In reality, it appears the posting was an indication of God's favor. Patrick noted that his dearest friend first told him, "Look, you are to be raised to the rank of bishop."

Sometime before his arrival in Ireland and perhaps to finance his journey, he sold his noble rank "without shame or regret, for the benefit of others." Patrick described most things in a matter-of-fact fashion, but the way he almost casually described this significant act speaks at once of his inner transformation, his impetuousness, and his disregard for social standing.

The traditional date of his arrival in Ireland was recorded as AD 432, though many believe it was as much as fifty years later.

His Effect

There is much else we could say about Patrick. By his own admission, he made many mistakes. He said, "I must return unending thanks to God who often pardoned my folly and carelessness," and also noted that he was given "so much grace." He may have had connections with the dreamy Irish, but was also a man with a large vision. He said of his task in the *Confession*, "It was then most necessary to spread out our nets so that a very great multitude might be caught for God..." He may have been relational, but not always nice. He was able to confront when necessary. No one who hoped to effect change in the warlike Irish could be faint of heart. In his *Confession*, he noted being in life-threatening danger twelve times and being rescued from numerous conspiracies (the details of which he says would bore us). These adventures confirmed that he had the wherewithal to confront ordinary people and leaders when necessary.

Much is written of Patrick outside of the primary documents, and much of it is certainly beyond the realm of fact. He likely did not chase the snakes from Ireland, nor did he necessarily use the shamrock to communicate the gospel. One story that may have a grain of truth to it tells how Patrick confronted the Irish king of Meath at the time of the pagan Feast of Beltane and the spring equinox while the king was lighting the great festival fire at Tara, the traditional site of Irish authority. Tara, even today in ruins, is a site that remains laden with a sense of spirituality and significance. It seems more than a hill. Instead, it seems the focal point of spirituality for the region. Near Tara is another hill, the hill of Slane, where during the same feast, in defiance of the authority of Tara and the law that no fire should be lit in the vicinity, Patrick lit his own ceremonial fire, commemorating Easter. To a king, a competing fire on an adjacent hill was not a welcome sight, and surprisingly a confrontation ensued that was only verbal and from which Patrick emerged unscathed. The Irish king was likely as impressed with his bravery as with his telling of the gospel. It was the start of the society's recognition of a higher authority, and if this story is not true, then stories similar to it must be, for Patrick was not one to avoid confrontation and nothing less than that kind of direct style would have won the Irish respect so quickly.

Whatever Patrick said to the Irish would have most certainly resonated with their ancient ways. Patrick had many tendencies in common with the Irish and toward the end of his life considered himself one of them. To communicate with them he would have likely focused on the transcendent aspects of the gospel. He would have brought new meaning to the loveliness they desired while identifying with their predicaments. He would have countered the troubling aspects of Irish society, those that related to human sacrifice and those that had connections with the occult. But, despite all their problems, Patrick did not completely dismantle the Irish beliefs.

The longest of the biblical quotes Patrick places in his *Confession* occurs just before he asks the question, "How could the Irish transform in such an astounding way?" It's a prophetic quote from Joel describing the new covenant: "And afterward, I will pour out my Spirit on all people. Your sons and daughters will prophesy, your old men will dream dreams, your young men will see visions. Even on my servants, both men and women, I will pour out my Spirit in those days." This is the clearest indication that Patrick saw the new covenant as a pivotal part of his work.

The last record we have of Patrick's life comes from Annal 493 of the *Annals of the Four Masters*. For the year noted as the Age of Christ, 493, the fifteenth year of Lughaidh, it provides this summary of his life:

> Patrick, son of Calphurn, son of Potaide, archbishop, first primate, and chief apostle of Ireland, whom Pope Celestine the First had sent to preach the gospel and disseminate religion and piety among the Irish, was the person who separated them from the worship of idols and spectres, who conquered and destroyed the idols which they had for worshipping; who had expelled demons and evil spirits from among them, and brought them from the darkness of sin and vice to the light of faith and good works, and who guided and conducted their souls from the gates of hell (to which they were going), to the gates of the kingdom

of heaven. It was he that baptized and blessed the men, women, sons and daughters of Ireland, with their territories and tribes, both fresh waters and sea inlets. It was by him that many cells, monasteries, and churches were erected throughout Ireland; seven hundred churches was their number. It was by him that bishops, priests, and persons of every dignity were ordained; seven hundred bishops, and three-thousand priests was their number. He worked so many miracles and wonders, that the human mind is incapable of remembering or recording the amount of good which he did upon the earth. When the time of St. Patrick's death approached, he received the Body of Christ from the hands of the holy Bishop Tassach, in the 122nd year of his age, and resigned his spirit to heaven.

Later Life

There were oddities surrounding the end of Patrick's life. Despite this glowing record in the annals, few of those who came immediately after him and seem influenced by his work mentioned his name. There is no word of him in the life of St. Brigid by Cogitosus, nor in St. Columbanus's writings, though the latter states definitely that his country had first received the faith from the Romans. Many consider this lack of reference reason to doubt the broadness of Patrick's influence, but it seems, rather, to confirm the extent of his ostracism at life's end.

Patrick was not a cerebral convert, but a transformed person. His success must have irritated those who thought themselves more qualified than him. His success likely ignited the jealousy of religious and establishment opponents who then attempted to discredit him. His *Confession* was written for a purpose. Patrick was self-conscious in his writing, having not learned proper Latin while captive, and he did not yearn to put pen to paper. He was forced to write to defend himself against those who accused him.

He says he was put on trial by a number of his seniors who came to cast up his sins against him. These would have been remnant church leaders in Britain, detached from Rome yet still exercising local influence. They would have said of him, "Why does this fellow throw himself into danger among enemies who have no knowledge of God?" They were eventually effective in discrediting him by rummaging through his past and unearthing something of a boyhood offense that he had confessed to his dearest friend, likely in Gaul. Most troubling to Patrick was that this was the same friend who first told him of his posting as bishop who now stood as his accuser.

Joseph Duffy says the stated charge against Patrick, his boyhood sin, sounds strange to our ears, but was fully consistent with the thinking on penance and the clerical discipline of the period. Patrick did not mention the sin, and to modern ears we imagine something horrific to produce such a backlash. In the fifth century, however, the sin need not have been great. We talked earlier of how the church has been slow to adopt new-covenant ideas on the forgiveness of sin and, in Patrick's day, anyone who was a penitent (had confessed a significant sin) was not eligible for the clergy, even if he had since reformed. It would be as serious as a police officer today having a drug trafficking charge unearthed from the past.

The charge against Patrick of having a past sin was a serious attempt to terminate his mission and remove him from office. We are not told his sin or the result of the trial. Patrick said he did not come out of it badly considering the disgrace and shame he felt. He wrote that his good standing was approved in the presence of God and the people. But he also wrote that he was deprived of his good name. As is the case with all smear campaigns, whether successful at making their case or not, the perception of a damaged reputation often is what remains in people's minds.

Patrick remained in Ireland and, in his *Confession*, he attempted to restore his reputation, but because of the discrediting of his character that resulted from the process of the trial, he died in rejection by his religious peers both at home and abroad. "For a century and a half after his own lifetime Patrick was ignored by the people he served so faithfully. Even when we allow for the scarcity of records and the difficulty of interpreting the sources that survive, this absence of profile has a firm basis in fact and seems to be quite deliberate."[8]

Patrick's repudiation is an example of the spiritual battle that followed him into his old age and an example of the kind of opposition that confirms that he lived his life, to some extent, outside of the religious mold of the time. The strength of opposition against him marks him as a pioneer. He was not shaped by the thinking around him. Rather, as a successful pioneer, his life and work ultimately survived the opposition he faced and resulted in a number of legacies. One of those legacies is the establishment of the private and confidential confessional. This Irish practice, that doubtless was instituted to protect others from the grief Patrick experienced, was eventually adopted by the entire church and one for which many now reap a benefit of peace and sanity. Further, if not for the accusations against him, we would likely only recognize Patrick in a mythical manner. The opposition he faced was petty and destructive yet most certainly drove him to write his *Confession* and, thus, the events in his later life confirm the power of God to work good out of evil and use it for our benefit by leaving material of substance for us to study.

What is particularly amazing about Patrick is that despite the climate created by his accusers, a climate that was based on establishing an unrealistic standard of perfection, he chose in his *Confession* to confirm that he made foolish mistakes and relied on grace. He defended himself while at the same time refusing the rules of their game. To me, this confirms that Patrick was intentional and purposeful—a man who had a focused message to deliver with his words and his life.

The most curious yet instructive thing about Patrick's mission is the opposition he faced. Patrick accomplished some revolutionary things in Ireland. He instigated a cultural transformation that resulted in the overthrow of the powerful within Irish society and left that society significantly altered.

People generally resist change, so one would think that sparking such a revolution would produce some lasting enemies from within. Yet, we see little of that. The Irish transformation had some internal opponents. Patrick related of the numerous (twelve) times God rescued him when his life was in danger. That danger was undoubtedly generated by those allied with druids, yet, in his retelling, that opposition seemed insignificant. It seemed localized to his early life and only warranted a footnote in his life story. The lack of opposition from the Irish Celts evidenced their hunger for change prior to Patrick's arrival.

People also generally revert back to their former ways after a superficial experience of change, so one would think that sustaining such a societal transformation—unless it was one built on some real internal change—would necessitate dealing with lingering enemies—the remnant saboteurs who want to return society to its preexisting state. Yet these saboteurs also do not seem to exist. After Patrick starts the cultural landslide, it continues on for generations with little internal opposition. The Irish welcomed the change. The lack of ongoing opposition demonstrated the internal reality of the transformation they experienced.

The true opposition Patrick eventually faced came not from within Irish Celtic society, or from remnant Irish. Instead, it came from a group of jealous religious cronies on an adjacent island. These religious clerics nominally shared the same faith as Patrick, but subversively resisted him and his work.

Why?

CHAPTER 6

SIMILARITIES BETWEEN US AND THE IRISH

RELIGION: LIKE THE cronies who opposed Patrick, it serves as a contrast to the new covenant—the polar opposite, the antithetical "other." Sometimes it is hard to believe that something so socially acceptable, so ubiquitous, so blandly helpful could really be the enemy. Is religion what opposes the kind of life Patrick described, even today?

I can start to answer that question with my own experience. Early in my life, church was the dominant structure. The sights, sounds, and smells of the church building return to my memory with more clarity than those same features of my childhood home. The place we called church, for me, was a community center, social house, and religious sanctuary. There we gathered to socialize, met before outings, compared cars, and, on Sunday, heard sermons. At times we would focus on religious promise and sing triumphant songs about glory, and at times we would hear sermons filled with superlatives describing God's beauty. I connected with the beauty and perfection those words conveyed. Yet, at other times, the words felt exaggerated and the superlatives turned sour. Oddly, the words of beauty seemed to morph into a paralyzing list of rules that we could not keep. Like the Irish, words from the Bible often felt like an Irish geis we lived under and a cloud that hung over us. We

The Irish and the Blank Page

accepted the reality of the system we found ourselves living in even though, at some level, we recognized its serious limitations and the lack of benefit it provided for us.

When I move past the stereotypical images of pagan druids, I realize the spiritual atmosphere in which the pre-contact Irish Celts operated bears a striking similarity to my experience in church. For them, a seemingly benevolent entity promised life and beauty, yet somehow ended up delivering restriction and fear—in spades—supposedly for the good of the people being enslaved. In my world, the benevolent entity was God: always portrayed as good, but never entirely good. Likewise, the promise of life and beauty was always slightly beyond reach. It rarely materialized.

In its absence, what sprouted was a garden of performance-based weeds that left me feeling inadequate and guilty for never quite having done enough. When I occasionally measured up to the standard—for example if I had done some volunteer work, read my Bible, or spoken to someone about my faith—rather than feeling joy, I would feel exceptional and aloof. And either way, whether I performed well or not, I didn't get the reality I sought. I remained detached from a sense of the transcendent beauty of the spiritual world. I did not taste the glory of God that surrounds us all. Those things were probably bombarding me, but instead of relishing in them, I was experiencing a choking sense of self-management. I was focused on something that crowded out all the beauty. In that state, I shared the predicament of those living in an Iron-Age agrarian world under the dominion of druids. We both were trapped and almost wholly distracted from the life we sought.

I love all things Irish: the beer, the uilleann pipes, the rock bands, the countryside, and I wonder about the reasons for this attraction. Perhaps it's no more than one in a collection of preferences that any one person assembles. But, after studying Patrick and the Celts, another more likely reason has become particularly clear: I believe I relate to the Irish because I share some of the same beginnings as they did. We have a very different set of external circumstances. Yet the similarity is there. The Irish were, and are, inescapably spiritual. They were one of the few pagan cultures who erected a lovely spirituality and became focused on achieving that loveliness in practice. Their world was framed with the promise of beauty, yet in practice their world was filled with restrictions, taboos, and fear. My early world was similarly framed.

The similarity between my world and theirs requires some further discussion. My world operated with the benefits of technology and is built on a theology that has been honed over centuries; theirs operated out of a pantheistic and primitive belief system that also may have been honed over centuries. The similar results produced—despite the centuries that separate us—suggests that humanity, in some ways, has made little progress in fifteen hundred years. And that lack of progress can be a disturbing thought.

The reasons for that lack of progress? Maybe we moderns think too much of ourselves, maybe we suffer from a lack of humility—or lack of effort—or maybe we are more tradition bound than we imagine. Maybe we are just unwilling to progress. To me, the commonality of our experience across centuries, more than reinforcing some specific weakness of ours, suggests a common force that opposes us. It suggests that for most of us only a few primary distractions conspire to keep us from life. The branches of those distractions may have different features but they share the same roots. It also suggests that our opponent is relatively oblivious to what we consider significant weapons. Neither our modern technological prowess nor the sophistication of the religious system we live under makes much difference in the ability of this distraction to take hold.

This distraction is not unique to churches such as the one I grew up in. Whether you attend a church, mosque, or synagogue, you have likely experienced this same distracting tendency. It's like a dark backdrop to the peace, serenity, and fulfillment that religious services advertise. It makes us all subservient to rules, reduces our perspective, and sets us up to make comparisons with each other. We could argue about which version of the backdrop is darkest, but instead we will consider the darkness of the backdrop as a useful contrast. We will consider it as a shadow behind the new covenant. If we study that shadow, we may get a better picture of what constitutes the light.

Religion

We'll use the word *religion* to describe the ubiquitous shadow with Iron-Age roots, and accept the negative casting of this word. And we'll look at religion mainly for the purposes of helping define the new covenant. We'll use "authentic faith" to generically describe the opposite: faith that connects with the true God and produces indisputably positive results in a person's life and in the lives of others around him or her.

With that casting of the word, we can hopefully put down our defenses. To the degree your experience contained, or contains, religious elements, you can be angry at those elements that have robbed you of life. To the degree that your experience includes authentic faith alongside the religiosity it toils under, you can acknowledge the good and accept it as somehow surviving amongst thorns. Our goal, don't forget, is not to defend the status quo, but to look at what holds us from experiencing that life-shaking reality that transformed the Irish.

How do you define religion? Dictionaries define it as any system or institution with which you engage to foster a sense of meaning or relevance in relation to something greater than yourself. They define the organized version as something in which rules exist to govern the means by which adherents participate in the religion. Those definitions may help a bit, but may also raise further debate about what is at the core of religion. We'll talk about that core, but first let's define a religious structure by what it produces.

Religion produces a number of negative internal by-products: insubstantiality, performance orientation, a culture of lies. We will review those in some detail, but let's start with first impressions. To me, religion always tends toward exclusivity and has a way of making people feel awkward. It likes to stay hidden, like the embarrassing drinking habits of your relatives. It's something you tend to not bring into the light of conversational day for some reason. Maybe that's because religion is no longer socially acceptable and its vocabulary is not common outside the fold. Maybe it's because religion is dark and prefers dark places. Or maybe it's because you can't make many good stories from religious topics. If you do manage to do so, say at a party, you probably also manage to alienate at least one other person in the room. Your religious experience might be nice and kind, but your religious conversation will often reveal or expose scars of some sort in others. Those others likely have had a difficult history with religious institutions and when you open the topic of religion, you discover that you rarely do so starting from a clean slate.

Words that sound like religion have to overcome hurdles before reaching minds and hearts in our culture. When we do find an environment where we can speak openly about an agency that has exercised control over our thoughts and lives, many of us find ourselves expressing excessively. I've ranted. Perhaps you've ranted too. As I write this, I'm aware of a number of anti-religious books that recently populated the shelves of bookstores. The titles are not friendly. One was *The End of Faith*, another was subtitled, *How Religion Poisons Everything*, and yet another one was *Breaking the Spell*. What these titles confirm is that others are ranting too. Religion may be awkward, but it remains a significant force in our world and continues to evoke strong emotions.

The titles I mentioned indicate a strong undercurrent of negative passion against religion. I've read most of these books, and while they're not powerful polemics, they do present all religion as dangerous and foolish superstition—something from the dark past; something to be abandoned, quickly. They also suggest discarding the concept of God and faith entirely because of the religious havoc wreaked in the past. Is that a reasonable thing to do?

I know from personal experience that losing your religion—of the sort we've just defined—is like freeing yourself from a tyrant and walking out of jail. Upon seeing the sunshine, you feel a sense of joy followed by a natural resentment for having been taken captive for so long—often not so much by physical force, but rather by the ability of religion to get inside your head and bend your will with its power. You've been made a willing slave. Some ranting is justifiable.

Religion operates by getting inside your head. It works through an insidious process. The process is the same whether utilized by church leaders or druids. The process begins with leaders who gain authority by claiming a connection to the highest order. This connection allows the leaders to discourage dissension, always claiming virtue, thus placing themselves beyond criticism. They focus on performance so the culture created is negative, but leaders amplify the smallest bit of positive reinforcement within the group—someone gives a positive testimony—and use it to validate the entire system. There is a promise of life coupled with punishment for disobedience. Together, these motivators constitute a powerful force from which it is difficult to break free without outside support.

The life ultimately promised by religion can seem wonderfully appealing, but there are always gatekeepers who broker this life. These gatekeepers adopt surprisingly similar methods for restricting entry into the Promised Land—whether they are druids or clergy. They make the promised life achievable mainly through self-denying effort. They deliver confusing messages so that the promised life seems strangely insubstantial, and they don't seem to care if the process they create becomes defeating and isolating. This for me was accomplished by pastors that half-heartedly preached God's grace and wholeheartedly preached an obligation to serve God and perform spiritual disciplines. The result was not balance—it was defeat.

At its core, the dynamic within religion that confuses, restricts access to, and dilutes the truth seems cultic and primitive. Further, scratching beneath the surface it always seems to reveal a surprising amount of evil in the lives of the perpetrators. When, by some means, you find yourself free from its power you feel as though a bubble has popped and what was clouded becomes clear. The characteristics of the system you thought normal now seem absurd. You may even rant.

Insubstantiality

Of the negative characteristics a religious system produces, the foremost is lack of solidity. The Irish knew a lack of solidity resulting from the possibility of shape-shifting. Their world was not confirmed as solid. It was not able to be tested. It was not able to be found faulty or to be found reliable. Things, people, and creatures were subject to unexpected change. That change was not predictable; rather it was precarious. Because the Irish world was precarious, their outlook on life was highly dependent on the interpreters—dependant on those who may have control over the uncertainty and those who could explain its precariousness. The Irish people were dependent.

This precariousness also created an outlook that was fearful of unexpected possibilities. They could not trust the universe enough to independently test the world for themselves. The world was not solid enough for that kind of approach. They didn't test and rely on nature as we do every day. We take for granted our laws of science and probability, which rely on a sense of evenhandedness in the world. They coped with a changeful world—they dreamed and they listened to those who claimed to understand the unfathomable.

The dependency, fear, and lack of trust hampered their ability to explore the world around them. In a way it caused much of their world to disappear. The world became less substantive and less lovely. The insidious system had a way of making the real world insubstantial.

In most churches, the lack of solidity presents itself through what appears to be a deliberate inconsistency in teaching. God is generally presented as good, and that goodness woos people. But he's not always good. Every once in a while a statement or presentation of his nature pulls the rug out from under the adherents. Amidst the sermons on love, there comes a tough sermon that leaves the listeners without stability. I know this feeling well, and after recognizing it, have come to resent it. It's not that I expect God to be fully definable or simple to understand or even always good in my estimation. There is an understandable element of mystery to God. But I don't expect immature, angry, destructive, petty, or controlling depictions of him. The result of those kinds of messages makes God seem unpredictable and makes his followers troubled because at some level we wonder whether we've committed our lives to a monster.

The Irish and the Blank Page

When religious leaders communicate God's supposed dark side, I believe they do it under a sort of duress, and it seems they go through predictable motions beforehand. If you've heard as many sermons as I have, you recognize those predictable motions. On the morning of a tough sermon, the body language is stiffer, faces are sterner, and smiles are less broad. The bodily affectations reflect the inner detachment that has to occur in order to deliver the harsh, abusive message that's about to come—the message that's brutal, but supposedly true; the message that contradicts much of what they otherwise say and do; the message that says something like God delivers sickness, death, or pain for our own good. C. S. Lewis describes this detachment in his book *The Pilgrim's Regress*.

John, the protagonist and pilgrim of the story, is young and longs to know the truth about the world. He's brought by his parents at a young age to see the village elder, who's called the steward and who represents the ultimate religious figure, the Landlord. Lewis captures the mixed messages given by the steward—the strange smiling preamble, the constant references to the Landlord's kindness in and amongst his threats of destruction. The steward displays many of the same dissociative mechanisms I noticed in pastors. He uses a mask in front of his face, he goes into a set of rituals, he changes his voice. All these act as a sort of survival mechanism—a way of dealing with the contradictions they're about to deliver without going insane.

What emerges out of the dissociation in the minds of the listeners is a strange mix of loyal belief in an age-old system, no matter how harsh and unbelievable, and a sort of shared agreement toward unbelief. The shared unbelief is summarized by Lewis when, after the long and frightening discussion, John sincerely asks what he should do. The steward responds rather cheerily, "I wouldn't worry about it too much at all if I were you." The inconsistency in the message reduces the central focus of the religious organization to insubstantiality. Like the Irish shape-shifters, it makes the world disappear.

There are many ways miscommunication of truth can make the physical world disappear. In my early church days, the world partly disappeared because of a weighty sense of balance. If I had

Similarities Between Us and the Irish

a good time doing something or at a gathering, I would need to balance it with some study or meditation. Fun always required balance by discipline; leisure required balance by work. The balance helped me continue feeling good about myself. But the good feeling was unsustainable and the sense of self-management was palpable—as was the corresponding lack of joy. I did not experience the transcendent beauty of the spiritual world. I did not taste the glory of God or the grace that surrounds us all. Those things were probably bombarding me, but my focus on measuring up and desire for balance crowded all that out.

My church, like most religious groups, did not suggest my preoccupation with something that was defeating life—in my case balance—was irregular or unhealthy. Rather my experience seemed quite in keeping with other people's lives. Church, in general, seemed filled with superlative language, but mundane and often unhealthy experience. "That's the way it is," I thought.

That's what the Irish must've thought as they accepted that the beauty was for someone else, but the burden was for them. If the desired results weren't obtained, the root cause was likely that someone wasn't doing something right. Religious teachers, or druids, are never wrong and so the fault always lies with the subjects, the people who are not carrying the load.

The process of creating insubstantiality is insidious. It doesn't go for frontal attacks; rather, like shape-shifting, it blends opposites together and removes their distinctiveness. Through that process it achieves the impossible. Normally, there is a sharp contrast between an authentic spiritual life and a church-bound life: one life is filled with joy and a sense of abandon, and one is filled with burdens. They are patently different—like the difference between a shard of broken glass and a diamond. If the two are ever side by side the difference is readily apparent. But diamonds certainly are rare and they don't often stand side by side with the shards. Because the duller shards of glass typically stand alone they can, through an insidious process, eventually be thought of as diamonds.

We can actually become convinced of the similarity. We will even develop rationale to defend the similarity. Both shine—to a degree. Both are transparent—to a degree. Both have edges. When you look at the shard of glass long enough, and get told the right words at the same time, you start to believe that diamonds are nothing more than those shards. You start to believe this similarity even though diamonds are full of beauty and usefulness and shards of glass are plain, simple, worn out, and often dangerous. The most powerful ability of religion is to make the real disappear.

Performance

Another characteristic of a religious system is holding out the promise of life only to those who achieve it through self-denying effort. This rationale doesn't sound all that bad at first. Life is good; go earn it. This rationale may even sound good to those who don't need help, aren't weak, and are capable and can make things work. In fact, this thinking has a strong appeal to a hard-working, successful culture and has an especially strong and twisted appeal to those (like the Irish) drawn to achieve perfection.

The effort is couched in terms that make it sound positive. Sometimes it's called "service," and those who excel at serving are held in the highest esteem. The tempting foundation of all the effort is self-sufficiency. Underpinning the foundation is the idea that we can impress deity, we can manage our world, we can keep the system going, we can keep the necessary rules, and we can somehow fit the whole spiritual puzzle together on our own. Something so based in personal effort and hard work is hard to denounce in our culture. But eventually the appeal of hard work becomes the only appeal. In these spiritual cultures, hard work becomes virtually idolized, and grace—the energizing power behind the new covenant—becomes an anathema. These cultures generally don't grow; and if they continue, they end up rehearsing their past and generally experiencing decline.

On the performance treadmill the effort required to measure up sometimes heads toward the extremes of self-denial. Self-denial fragrantly flaunts the original aim of the system—to pursue life—and instead leads people toward a merciless reduction of life. Life is denied: the ultimate shape-shift. Of course, some level of self-denial can achieve a greater good in the longer term. Medical students toil long hours for low pay because they know their reward is coming. But the religious system honors self-flagellation for no other purpose than to somehow satisfy the demands of deity and prove piety.

At one time I had a lot of effort invested in my religious life, including two years of full-time religious schooling and a life of striving. I had made an effort—gone on mission trips, built houses for others, sacrificed my time and money. For all my expenditures I had less than I wanted both in terms of tangible results and personal satisfaction. I often just lay on my bed feeling paralyzed and thinking I had more to do but was not sure what it was. The performance culture is never satisfied.

For some, like me, words from spiritual leaders carry significant weight and, for various reasons, the doors leading to escape, denial, or abstraction open only in a very narrow way. The only option the performance culture seems to leave open is the way of emphasizing defeat. Those who recognize the loftiness of the standard and realize they don't measure up get left with an internal message of defeat, and the message produces shame and isolation. Shame and isolation make relating to others difficult. It's entirely inhuman.

Not only relational weakness, there are a host of other somewhat juvenile characteristics that a religious system fosters, and they all, to some degree, serve as a dark background to the new covenant because of the tendency they have to devalue people—especially those who don't perform or measure up. The devaluation stifles relationships, both between people and between people and God.

At its core, religion has a goal to confirm that your life and your deeds are right, rather than wrong—and that by implication you are good (or becoming good), rather than bad. Right versus wrong is the fuel that drives the system. And it does produce some seemingly positive results—they are just not new-covenant results. Money is raised, people are assisted, but the negative relational by-products of living under a system with a primary goal of confirmed rightness are staggering. What typically results from this culture is an atmosphere in which people find themselves in a mode of self-promotion and comparison. Authentic expression and real human connection become secondary to confirming rightness. It becomes, at some core level, a false society.

Falsehood

In a new-covenant culture we accept our desperate need for God, and admit our failures because we realize they aren't going to provoke wrath. We honestly rely on God's grace. When performance is the agenda, however, people hide their fallibility and weakness. In a performance culture a few people set the standard based on their natural abilities, the rest hide their weakness through various falsifications. They deny their problems exist, rationalize their potential for harm, and philosophize away their existence. It's the only alternative to constantly admitting defeat, which we are loathe to do.

So religious groups, being performance oriented, become places that harbor and promote falsehood. It is odd that a highly moralistic group that overtly has little tolerance for lies will willingly nurture falsifications. But the higher cause—the need to perform—governs, so the falsehood continues. It's a by-product.

The agreement in, or shared, falsehood happens in major or surprising ways. I was personally shocked when I eventually discovered what was going on behind the scenes in my church. Every man came to church in suits and ties and every woman in a nice dress in those days. They presented well on Sundays, but many of those well-dressed exteriors were in shambles on the inside. I never heard talk of the affairs, the molesting, the inner pain, and the disarray.

Shared falsehood happens in other more subtle ways. While we deny and falsify our own pain we simultaneously cast ourselves as set apart from outsiders. Most religious groups are quite clear about the need to keep those who do not conform on the outside. Words like *pagan, atheist, unbeliever, infidel,* and even *liberal* all serve to label outsiders. The more severe these distinctions between "us" and "them" the more narrow, isolated, and conspiratorial a group becomes. The labeling and distinction shrinks the group and makes it less appealing. Nevertheless we overlook this painful liability and can't see the harm in excluding the majority of humankind. This distinction is largely a falsehood because the biggest common bond that humanity shares is the need of grace. But casting ourselves as "set apart" somehow seems genuinely right and even seems more right when we place a lot of emphasis on winning converts. This seems paradoxical, but it works. You can psychologically allow yourself to exclude most of society if you also work hard to convince outsiders to join your group. Of course, they will need to adopt your beliefs and conform to your code first.

The unspoken rationale could be phrased simply as, "We don't want you now, but if you would change we would welcome you with open arms." In this sense, proselytizing serves a group need. Often religious groups will overtly rank the winning of converts as their ultimate priority, but the actions (and dollars) of the group do not support this. Rather, in religious structures, the purpose of placing a high value on winning converts is to relieve the guilt associated with excluding so much of society. I believe people need Jesus. We all need Jesus, though, and the new covenant is about inclusion. We often maintain exclusive attitudes that have more to do with the pride of the religious system than with the truth.

Once we falsify our lives we move to falsifying who we are, then proceed to falsify what God says and who he is. This becomes a false culture. It can't survive without complicity, so the falsification becomes embedded. Those who speak the truth get marginalized or ostracized.

This is extremely insidious. It starts off seeming very minor and winds up like a toxic fog. In almost every rebuke that Jesus levied at the Pharisees he used the word *hypocrites*. They were not real. They had somehow come to terms with being profoundly duplicitous. Falsehood is the toxic product of the religious environment. And so, for many reasons, these communities become people of the mask. They hide behind smiley faces and other forms of pretension and falsehood and leave their hidden pain and angst covered. We all wear masks to a certain extent. When you nod and smile at the person in the seat beside you before a flight takes off, you expect a masked response that's appropriate for acquaintances. Most people's masks, however, are of the papier-mache variety: they're crude, they don't stick well, and they come off easily. Religion takes those everyday masks and puts them through a kiln (the culture of harboring lies) so they come out hard and glossy and perfect in a hideous sort of way.

Before we consider the major obstacle people face when moving away from religion, consider what the poet Rumi says: "Out beyond ideas of wrongdoing and rightdoing there is a field. I will meet you there."[1] That simple statement—which resonates with Paul's statement, "Love keeps no record of wrongs"[2]—suggests we can only meet and connect honestly with each other in a place that transcends performance. We come to realize that's true in our important relationships, yet it's hard to imagine that kind of spiritual place—especially when we've been socialized in a world that focuses on right and wrong. But that's the kind of territory God imagined when he created the new covenant. And so the core goal of authentic spiritual life is strikingly different from the core goal of a religious life. The core goal of spiritual life recognizes that life itself has inherent value. Thus the goal of authentic spiritual life is simply to get as much of the life offered as possible. There's almost an element of greed in it. There's nothing religious about it. Jesus tells the story of a man who sells everything he has to get that life. Spiritual reality has a strong appeal, and, oddly enough, if you have a goal of getting something inherently good in as big a dose as possible you set yourself on a self-correcting process.

Loyalty

So why don't more people focus on getting that life and turn from religion? They are retained through a sense of loyalty to an age-old institution. In this sense, I draw parallels between religious institutions and railroad companies. I don't mean to cast aspersions on railways, but there are similarities. They're both historic institutions. They're both solid and inflexible. The creeds and dictates of religion usually have arisen from historic events, like divine revelation, martyrdom, historic meetings, or battle. So they're beyond question. Railways are also inflexible. They own a narrow strip of land that they've acquired over the course of history. They've laid their tracks on that land and they have ownership and rights to that route. Their pathways are fixed by past decisions; their current and future territorial options are limited. They, like religions, and by nature, are inflexible and protective organizations. The stone-hardened and weather-worn buildings of both institutions seem purposely fashioned to remind you that the organization behind them carries the burgeoning weight of history.

Whereas railroads protect themselves by maintaining and preserving tracks and territory, religions protect themselves by maintaining and preserving a system of thought and usually an associated set of rules. That's their agenda. Whether the agenda stands the test of time, or whether the agenda continues to work, or whether the agenda helps others eventually ceases to matter. What matters is whether you promote the agenda or not. If you do—you're accepted. If you don't, then you are on the outside.

The historic nature of religious institutions attracts loyalty. All organizations require some level of loyalty. If you work for a company, for example, you keep their secrets and honor non-competition clauses. Likewise, if you live in a nation, you belong to that nation and if you divulge its secrets, you are guilty of treason. Without loyalty, you don't belong. You're a mercenary or hired gun or an independent. Religious loyalty is like the loyalty of everyday organizations, only deeper and more entrenched. Whereas people may feel trapped by their commercial loyalties, those same people will give themselves voluntarily to their religious loyalties and not consider breaking their loyalty for anything. I've met people who don't go to church or practice much of their religion, but who retain an intense sense of connection with their religion and would not abandon it or sell its secrets any more than I would sell nuclear secrets to my country's enemies. They have a deep sense of religious loyalty. It's familial, hereditary, personal, and unwavering.

People stay with their religions for traditional reasons, but there are personal ones too. One of the most personal reasons for staying religious is that the alternative feels so uncontrolled and unpredictable. Religion serves many purposes, but a key need it fills is to remove much of the unpredictability from the God equation. Religion tries to tame God—to make a gelding from a stallion.

To know God you have to step into mysterious territory. You have to lose your religion. You can't let go halfway. Often people prefer the tame, neutered, and controlled version of God and (wrongly) believe that somehow that tame version will be less toxic than the God they must meet on his own terms. As we have seen, that process produces many negative side effects for the little comfort it gives.

Indicators

The religious system is so insidious that you may not even know you're involved in it without checking some indicators. One indicator that reveals you are embroiled in the performance-based culture is your language. The most prevalent word that comes out of the performance culture is the word *should*. The word has large appeal both inside and outside religious circles, but it has particular religious uses.

If I had my druthers, people would only be allowed a couple uses of the word *should* per year. It deserves restriction because it is so loaded with guilt and throws a wet blanket on the concepts of personal freedom and individual responsibility. You should pay your taxes; you should go to church; you should wash behind your ears. Why? Just because you're told to? Who's telling you? Do you have a choice? "Why has every man a conscience then?"[3] *Should* is a word that emphasizes our subservience to some unknown authority. It relies on guilt for compliance, such as, "You should call your mother." "Should" generally produces questionable results because of its questionable motivators.

It's not generally a necessary word either. All "should" statements can be replaced by "if" or "will" statements. If you don't call your mother, she will be angry; if you don't pay your taxes you will get a fine or go to jail. At least that rephrasing speaks of choice and consequence rather than strict obligation.

"Should" plays into religious schemes when it reinforces a weak sense of accepted noncompliance. Putting a should in our statements somehow allows us to declare mixed messages such as saying, for example, while eating a donut, "I should cut back on sugar" or while talking about someone else, "We shouldn't be gossiping." Should, in these instances, reinforces the cycle of obligation/noncompliance/guilt and actually brands the cycle as acceptable. If people spoke without "shoulds" and instead used "if, then" language they would address their harmful habits. For example, "If I keep eating sugar, I will definitely gain more weight." Or "If we keep gossiping, we will destroy our image of that person and lose our own freedom in the area we are criticizing." It would be hard to say either of those last two statements with the self-condoning smile that often accompanies a "should." Instead, "should" becomes a keystone of religious language: a word that accepts noncompliance, but adds guilt to compensate. Excessive "should-ing" creates an intolerable environment, and even infrequent usage has a unique power to suffocate life because of the way it appeals to unquestionable authority and removes choice.

Another indicator to consider when assessing your level of enmeshment in a religious culture is to ask yourself how much you rely on the opinions of others. Are you always looking over your shoulder? When you look closely at the religious web, you realize it's based on a culture of compliance rather than a culture of freedom and individuality. Haircuts are the same, attitudes are the same, and affiliations are the same. In many ways, a religious church is a lot like a high school full of teenagers. They are generally all the same and intent on becoming socialized into the culture of sameness rather than becoming individuals who can shape the culture.

The final indicator to consider is to ask yourself how much abundant life you are experiencing. Ongoing lack of vitality can be the ultimate driving force that generates the huge amount of courage it takes to break free from this entrenched system. You need enough courage to become a traitor to it.

We need a leader who speaks truth and offers hope if we are going to break free from religious oppression. That is what the Irish got with Patrick, and this is what the first-century Jews got with Jesus.

Jesus' searing words, "Woe to you, blind guides"[4] seem intentionally barbed to cause the religious bubble to pop and enable the courageous decision to break with what previously appeared as trusted religious institutions. Jesus also gave words of hope so that after the bubble burst and the venting was complete, there would be something left to hope for from God: "I am with you always."[5]

For us, the post-religious, there remains rational basis for hope. There is evidence that belief in God and faith in his existence, essential religious practice, can produce positive outcomes. I mentioned the Cahill lecture I attended while in San Francisco. During that same stay I also attended a lecture by a Helen Ellerbe, who had written a book called *The Dark Side of Christian History*. She documented the negative effects the church had on people throughout history: the witch hunts, the crusades, etc. It was in the same room as the earlier Irish lecture I mentioned, but this audience was decidedly post-religious and the question period was filled with venting. From where I sat in the audience, and in life, I felt able to ask only one question: "Was it all negative or did your research reveal anything positive about Christians in history?"

She responded passionately, saying that in the midst of horrible events such as the Salem witch trials, there was surprising evidence of Christians sheltering and hiding those accused—at great personal risk. In the midst of the persecution brought by religion, the reality of authentic faith surfaced. The darkest backdrop highlights the nature of the light.

For our purposes, the hopeful lesson that arises when properly considering the Irish and religion is that we can't reasonably discard the idea of God and faith. According to the Irish story, something with that label—church or religion—dramatically and positively transformed the Irish society into something civilized, improved, and worth replicating.

Patrick was a bishop but somehow not religious. He lacked the proper preparation to be religious. He wasn't highly educated, wasn't possessed with great skill at oratory; his training in entitlement was thankfully interrupted. He had none of the usual precedents to a religious life and seemed very uninterested in clinging to anything religious in later life. Look at Patrick's breastplate—a prayer, if not written by him, then surely influenced by his life. As you read it, consider how unreligious it is.

Similarities Between Us and the Irish

Patrick's Breastplate

I arise today
Through a mighty strength, the invocation of the Trinity,
Through belief in the threeness,
Through confession of the oneness
Of the Creator of Creation.

I arise today
Through the strength of Christ's birth with his baptism,
Through the strength of his crucifixion with his burial,
Through the strength of his resurrection with his ascension,
Through the strength of his descent for the judgment of Doom.

I arise today
Through the strength of the love of cherubim,
In obedience of angels,
In the service of archangels,
In hope of resurrection to meet with reward,
In prayers of patriarchs,
In predictions of prophets,
In preaching of apostles,
In faith of confessors,
In innocence of holy virgins,
In deeds of righteous men.

I arise today
Through the strength of heaven,
Light of sun,
Radiance of moon,
Splendor of fire,
Speed of lightning,
Swiftness of wind,
Depth of sea,
Stability of earth,
Firmness of rock.

I arise today

Through God's strength to pilot me:
God's might to uphold me,
God's wisdom to guide me,
God's eye to look before me,
God's ear to hear me,
God's word to speak for me,
God's hand to guard me,
God's way to lie before me,
God's shield to protect me,

God's host to save me
From snares of devils,
From temptation of vices,
From everyone who shall wish me ill,
Afar and anear,
Alone and in a multitude.

I summon today all these powers between me and those evils,
Against every cruel merciless power that may oppose my body and soul,
Against incantations of false prophets,
Against black laws of pagandom,
Against false laws of heretics,
Against craft of idolatry,
Against spells of witches and smiths and wizards,
Against every knowledge that corrupts man's body and soul,

Christ to shield me today
Against poison, against burning,
Against drowning, against wounding,
So that there may come to me abundance of reward.
Christ with me, Christ before me, Christ behind me,
Christ in me, Christ beneath me, Christ above me,
Christ on my right, Christ on my left,
Christ when I lie down, Christ when I sit down,
Christ when I arise,
Christ in the heart of every man who thinks of me,

Christ in the mouth of everyone who speaks of me,
Christ in every eye that sees me,
Christ in every ear that hears me.

I arise today
Through a mighty strength, the invocation of the Trinity,
Through belief in the threeness,
Through confession of the oneness
Of the Creator of Creation.

It's a fantastic prayer filled with action, connection with nature, recognition of battle, and most of all, it's a Christ-centered prayer. Consider how unlike it is to similar prayers of that same period.

You are great, LORD and highly to be praised, great is your power and your wisdom is immeasurable. Man, a little piece of your creation, desires to praise you, a human being "bearing his mortality with him" carrying with him the witness of his sin and the witness that you resist the proud. Nevertheless, to praise you is the desire of man, a little piece of your creation.[6]

It is admittedly odd to compare one's prayer to another's, but notice by comparison the earthiness, vitality, and lack of introspection of Patrick's prayer.

Our goal in this part of our exploration of the new covenant, and Patrick, is to disentangle the essential religious belief from the religious web with which it has become entwined. We need to do this with our lives as well. This is a rescue mission of sorts, a rescuing of the truth. Ask for help from God to carry out this mission in your life.

The charm of history and its enigmatic lesson consist in the fact that, from age to age, nothing changes and yet everything is completely different.

—Aldous Huxley

CHAPTER 7

EARLY IRISH CHARACTERISTICS

THE ANCIENT IRISH, who strove for beauty, loveliness, and who innately believed that God (or the spirit world) was filled with the same qualities, connected powerfully with the gospel—perhaps because they had one less barrier to cross. They were purists from the start. Patrick did not need to overcome any of their jaded disillusionment with the universe before introducing them to Jesus. I suspect that's true in general of people today. If you believe God is good, you're much more likely to connect with him powerfully. You are one step closer to the truth.

But the Irish also brought some baggage into their newfound relationship with God. Before receiving the gospel, the early Irish had let their desire for beauty and loveliness lead them into a web of rules and geasa. The pagan restrictions they developed on the road to beauty had unknowingly sidetracked them from their goals and produced bondage. We saw the Irish bondage in chapter 2. In this chapter, we want to look at how the Irish freedom took a healthy stance against that kind of bondage. We will look at the habits and ambitions the Irish developed after Christianity and see how those habits were a healthy reaction against their restrictive past.

When something, or someone, frees you from an abusive and controlling system, you often vow never to go near that territory again. The pendulum of your life swings and you don't so much straighten up as lean away from what you have been freed from. It may not be entirely healthy, but it's natural. And it's more natural when the restrictions have been severe. Before we leave the Irish, we want to take one last look at their uniquely Irish expressions of the Christian faith. We will look at their lives after the gospel for reactions in directions opposite of control.

One of the most significant features of ancient Irish Christianity was their attraction to the monastic or ascetic lifestyle. Asceticism was a growing part of the Roman church at the time. Just a few decades before Patrick's birth, Athanasius had published *The Life of St. Antony*, which described the life of the desert father and characterized his ascetic lifestyle in a way that appealed to many. What likely attracted many Irish to this new movement was the extreme flavor of Christianity it offered. It provided a means for the dedicated and passionate to express their faith in an intense way. The Irish, who naturally considered spirituality as part of their every moment, could not, it seems, ignore the call to dedicate their entire lives to God through denial and extreme commitment. Monastic commitments were thus welcomed by the Irish who were gripped by their spirituality and drawn to radical expressions of it.

In the Irish monasteries we see reactions against control of their past. Irish monasteries quickly became places that exercised an academic kind of tolerance. No book was forbidden to the monks. Other monastic traditions had restrictive reading lists, but the Irish monasteries refused to adopt practices that hinted of past restrictions. They believed that the truth could stand up to scrutiny and they also wanted nothing more to do with the forbidding of the written word, so they read voraciously and widely. It didn't matter if the book was considered sacred or profane. The Irish structured learning within their monastic system without taboos on the written word. This principle seems, to anyone familiar with Celtic history, an obvious one for them to adopt. But this freedom was not at all common in the larger religious or ascetic world. Those considered spiritual men at that time, such as St. Antony, read only the Scriptures. The freedom to read from various sources made the Irish scholars highly sought after as teachers. The Irish that wandered Europe later in the ninth century often served as teachers for children of nobility because they could teach all subjects. These Irish were scholars who had no fear of knowledge. Rather, they were those who had been freed from restrictive modes of thought and hence modeled freedom in their lives.

Removing restrictions on written material fostered a paradigm that in many ways helped to purge previously held distinctions. There were no taboos on so-called secular literature; there were no unreadable authors, no untouchables, no people beyond God's reach. The Irish were, like anyone who comes in contact with grace, freed from smallness of thought that creates distinction between peoples and freed into a perspective that sees the universe as God's kingdom. They had experienced a power that was real and transformational and so were not easily subjected to ideas that seemed alien to that power. Those who disagreed with their perspective were not a threat. They knew they stood in God's presence by grace and that anyone could reach that same standing, without effort. In that sense, they had come into contact with the new-covenant gospel—the great leveler of society.

This way of viewing society is highly indicative of an experience with the new covenant. It started with Jesus. He didn't exclude people. Jesus' lifestyle was broad. He associated with everybody: tax collectors, prostitutes, religious scholars, Pharisees, and fishermen. Jesus did not alter who he was; and if he did correct or rebuke, he did so openly, lovingly, and directly. Crowds felt welcome, included, and accepted. He could not afford to think or act in a small way—his task was to connect with all of Israel. He would fulfill Jeremiah's prophecy and bring knowledge of God to the houses of Israel and Judah from the least to the greatest.

People in Israel recognized how new inclusion was and the contrast to God's previous mode of operation. The sequence of covenants before Jesus can easily be seen as tools of exclusion. As God focused on specific groups, he also excluded more people from direct receipt of his blessing. In choosing Abraham, God excluded all the other families of the earth. In choosing Israel,

God excluded all other nations. Of course, there were exceptions. There usually are. God, through Jonah, reached out directly to the Assyrian Empire—even though his covenant at the time was to work through Israel. And God spoke to Nebuchadnezzar, the king of Babylon, in a dream. But in general, God's plan was to work through his chosen agency, Israel. When the tribe of Judah was chosen, the other 11 tribes were excluded. When David was chosen, Saul was excluded. By Jesus' time, the whole exercise of exclusion had been exhausted. It was as if God had expressed his frustration with mankind by sifting them through the covenants until none were left.

The feeling produced was despair. Jews, before Jesus, were in a post-religious age in terms of relationship with God. For them, the promises of the land, the blessings, and the eternal kingdom appeared to be gone. That arrangement hadn't worked. Both parties had the best of intentions, but there were irreconcilable differences. Like the Assyrian Empire before them and the Roman Empire after, the Hebrew Empire was fallen. The people meant to be a light to the nations had failed and now tasted bitter exclusion in their own mouths. Previous covenants had been called everlasting, but were now nullified. The results were real, the promises had evaporated, and God's exclusion produced a darkness and death. The chosen people were like the unchosen. Society had been leveled.

Into this level playing field, Isaiah writes of God:

> In a surge of anger I hid my face from you for a moment, but with everlasting kindness I will have compassion on you says the Lord your Redeemer. To me this is like the days of Noah, when I swore the waters of Noah would never again cover the earth. So now I have sworn not to be angry with you, never to rebuke you again.[1]

The new covenant more than restores Israel's previous status. It restores the kind of inclusiveness found in creation. It was for everybody, and it was good. Male, female, Jew, Greek, and we could add Catholic, Protestant, Liberal, Conservative, and more. John the Baptist introduced Jesus with, "All mankind will see God's salvation."[2] If this statement sounds disturbingly universalistic[3] to you then you should also know that it was a statement that was not fully comprehended by his Jewish audience. No one expected this would mean Gentiles might also inherit salvation. Even Jesus didn't go out of his way to include Gentiles. As the new-covenant age progressed, however, God increased their understanding through visions and the outpouring of his Spirit. Eventually, perhaps grudgingly, the church in Jerusalem accepted the fact that they were not "it" anymore. The gospel was out in the public domain, to be received and carried by all. Israel was the birthplace, but no longer the source. This truly was something new. The light was no longer held by a certain group or hindered by narrow founding statements.

If a club, religion, or business has a narrow founding statement, that statement will define the size of its audience and the scope of its influence. A founding statement with the fewest qualifiers has the largest potential. If your group has as a goal "to love the world," you could do anything anywhere, from building airplanes to counseling the troubled to feeding the hungry. However, if your goal is "to be the most efficient parts wholesaler in North America," you have more focus, but less potential. The new-covenant founding statement is just "Jesus." That statement can be expressed in so many ways to so many groups of people that it has limitless potential. It's not Jesus plus a church with traditions, or Jesus plus a smoke-free workplace—all those things may happen, but they are largely incidental to the essence.

It's not even Jesus plus Christianity. The tightly defined bounds that people place around Christianity have become a barrier to the inclusiveness that Jesus died to bring. We can't say what Jesus thought of Christianity—he didn't use the term. But whenever he spoke about his followers, he was clear that the bounds were fuzzy. The wheat and the tares would grow together. Jesus would make distinctions at the end of the age. For our age, Jesus' watchword is inclusion and a certain level of ignorance—mystery, if you will. But we don't like mystery, so we tend to turn Jesus into Christianity so we can properly exclude all those who don't subscribe to its bounded system. We've produced a vehicle of exclusion, and a hierarchy, when essential features of the new covenant are inclusiveness and a leveling, or equaling, of society.

Confession

Back to the Irish. Another distinctive of the early Irish church was the way they handled confession of sin. Christianity then and now is primarily viewed as a way to provide salvation from sin. The Irish were precocious enough to alter the means by which sin is confessed. Altering this process was tinkering with the stuff that appears to reside at the core of the faith. It was no small business. The fact that the Irish developed a unique (or new) aspect of confession evidenced a mindset within the Irish church that was willing to adopt newness in any area. It's a bold expression of the new covenant. The new features adopted in confession provided safeguards against those in authority and recognized an individual's value.

The Irish developed a distinctive, and previously unknown, form of confession that was made to a priest privately under the seal of secrecy. Likewise Irish priests prescribed the type of penance that could be performed by the confessor in private. Certain handbooks were made, called "penitentials," designed as a guide for confessors and as a means of regularizing the penance given for each particular sin.

Not only was this change boldly new, but it also most certainly traced its roots all the way back to Patrick's life and his negative experience with religious authorities who had betrayed his confidence. In that sense, it is also one of the reactions we are looking for—one of the ways their new lives were statements against their generally abusive past.

Prior to this adaptation, penance had been a public ritual. Penitents were divided into a separate part of the church and they came to mass wearing sackcloth and ashes in a process known as exomologesis that often involved some form of general confession. There is evidence that this public penance was preceded by a private confession to a bishop or priest, and it seems that, for some sins, private penance was allowed. Nonetheless, penance and reconciliation were prevailingly public rites (sometimes unrepeatable), which concluded with absolution or forgiveness.

This Irish adaptation recognized the personal nature of sin. In recognizing personal sin it also, in some sense, recognized the relative nature of sin that the apostle Paul described in his discussion on the purity of food (Rom. 14:14): "As one who is in the Lord Jesus, I am fully convinced that no food is unclean in itself. But if anyone regards something as unclean, then for him it is unclean."

In a way, the Irish adaptation of confession began the process of recasting sin to make our understanding of it consistent with the new covenant. It's personal, it's relative, and it's no longer a law-related issue. It remains toxic, but ceases to be the barrier it once was in our relationship with God. This process of recasting is entirely new, and for many churches is not yet complete.

We know that when reactive motion is nurtured for its own sake, it leads down a dead-end path. Yet we have seen that the reactive responses of Irish Christianity have great benefit in the life of a church. This oddity indicates the Irish people's encounter with God was much more than a reactive experience. Rather, it was authentic and life-giving. It had to have been authentic given how vibrant and long lived it was. Somehow the Irish found a way to not only react to their past, but also head toward the future. They headed in a direction that reconnected them with who they really were—apart from the control, the management, and the abuse.

Sin

Irish Christians did not get introspective and brooding about their sin. They also didn't ignore it. We just saw how they confessed it, but they also didn't spend a lot of time flagellating themselves for it. Their ancestors had been motivated by a search for beauty and it likely seemed appropriate to Patrick, and other leaders after him, that the Irish continue with that focus. They resisted promoting the battle with sin to the most senior of spiritual pursuits. The fact that they did so seems much more linked to their cultural heritage than to their theology, but it does suggest that they had little concern about the thought of God being angry with them. There was evil to fight and God, in the mind of the Celts, was capable of anger, but all God's anger was directed at the evil forces with which they were fighting and which opposed them. He wasn't angry with them for their latest transgression. In many ways the Celts' view of sin matches with new-covenant theology by "coincidence." They were culturally predisposed toward it.

For those of us with an introspective mindset, this view of sin and God's anger seems foreign. We often question, How could God not be angry? He was angry before, wasn't he? There is a story in the Old Testament book of Joshua in which a certain Hebrew named Achan was dragged out of his home—along with his sons and daughters, his cattle, donkeys, sheep, and all he had—to a public place. There, the whole family was stoned to death to appease God's wrath. That doesn't occur too often in my neighborhood. Has God become lax in judgment since then? Actually, in spite of what Achan suffered for his idolatry and greed, the Old Testament wasn't a period of thorough judgment. The purges were insufficient. The psalmist moans:

> O LORD, the God who avenges O God who avenges, shine forth. Rise up, O Judge of the earth; pay back to the proud what they deserve. How long will the wicked, O LORD, how long will the wicked be jubilant? They pour out arrogant words; all the evildoers are full of boasting…He will repay them for their sins and destroy them for their wickedness; the LORD our God will destroy them.[4]

Too much slipped through the cracks. The writer felt justice was not being done, even in the age of God's wrath. The wicked got away with too much. An eye for an eye was not carried out rigorously enough to produce any satisfaction. It also appeared the wrath wasn't producing much self-examination. Everything still focused on what was done to the author. The standard of justice and righteousness seemed too low. In spite of the brutality of Sodom and Gomorrah, that era was deficient to ours in terms of administering God's justice. To perfectly satisfy his own standard of righteousness, God would have had to kill everyone. Before the new covenant, justice was frustrated.

In these new-covenant days God has made judgment complete and thorough. He's become more consistent with the very basis of his nature. He's not angry. Our imperfections no longer anger him. No moral issues come between God and us and raise his ire or cause him grief. He acted like a grown-up and dealt with that dilemma directly and decisively. He removed sin by releasing his own Son to death. One of the most significant results of the new covenant can be expressed in the simple statement, "God is not angry with us." We can relax.

This is not easy to grasp—especially for a religious mind. It also is not entirely one dimensional. Is there a place for righteous anger? Yes. There may even be a brief time of wrath scheduled in God's timetable for the future. But things for the future are not the primary concern for those who want to fully experience the age in which we operate. You could say that the degree to which the statement "God is not angry" bothers you indicates the degree to which you have not embraced the new covenant. Take that response as good information and consider it. You may be able to rehearse verses and you may have interpretations that you have adopted that seem to reinforce God's current state of wrath. But when considering something new you need to start with the most valid reference point you have—yourself. Has God ever dealt in a wrathful way toward you? Have you ever come to him in prayer needing comfort and received wrath? Like me, you have probably been apprehended in your foolishness by God. Did he get your attention by communicating his wrath? If you answered those questions with a "No," (and I certainly did) and you continue to believe in God's anger, you must believe he is angry with others or, perhaps, poised to be angry with you in the future. Is that an objective position to take?

With your initial answer in mind, take the (rare) posture of a humble Pharisee—one who knows he or she may very well be guilty of significant biblical misinterpretation. Meditate on verses that communicate God's loving heart. You can temporarily put proof texts for God's anger on the shelf because you know you will never fully integrate all the verses of Scripture and you have a choice regarding what you begin to meditate on. You choose whether to meditate on essential new-covenant passages like the story of the prodigal son or passages like that of Ananias and Sapphira. They were the couple who promptly dropped dead in Peter's presence when he exposed their lie. Their isolated story is often brought up in defense of God's supposed continued anger, but a careful reading of the passage indicates suggestions of God's anger are completely implicit. In this story—like Jesus' story of the sheep and the goats, which we will look at later—the worst parts of the story are the parts we read into it, not what the story actually says. Now, as in Jeremiah's time, we need to recognize we can suffer under poor handling of the Word by others.[5]

If you want a passage to meditate on that reinforces our new-covenant position, consider the prophetic words of Isaiah chapter 54. This chapter follows a clear description of Jesus and what he came to do. Isaiah 53 passionately and poetically describes Jesus as he bravely inaugurates the new covenant. The next chapter, 54, describes the new-covenant environment. Its incredible promises include, in verse 9, the words we seem to need to hear over and over again: "So now I have sworn not to be angry with you, never to rebuke you again."

The Cross

When words fail us we use symbols. Symbols overcome challenges associated with multiple languages—hence their predominance in airports and assembly manuals—and the challenges associated with not having any written language. They effectively capture what words cannot. I chuckle every time I go into the Walnut Grove swimming facility in the Township of Langley. To complete it they arranged a small competition amongst primary students to develop signs and washroom symbols. This kind of focus on detail won the facility a number of architectural awards, and you can see why when you look at the stick figures that identify the shower rooms. They are only a few squiggles. They are so simple, so elementary, and so profound. They are not only joyful, the male figure is entirely male and the female figure essentially female. It's uncanny. That's the power of symbols: they communicate so much and do it across age and cultural boundaries.

Early Christians needed a symbol to convey the essence of their new faith. They first used the *ichthys,* or fish symbol, but later used the cross, and rightly so. The cross dominates all four gospel narratives and was the focus of Jesus' life. Yet for all its primacy, early Christians avoided it as a symbol, and for good reason. It was gruesome. The modern equivalent would be an electric chair.

I confess that like those early Christians I don't relish the cross or too much talk of it. Some people do. They give the cross a multi-dimensional presence that transcends space and time. It becomes sort of a clearinghouse where you can make spiritual transactions and go for comfort. That perspective doesn't seem incorrect but, to me, the cross speaks mostly of death and so I naturally keep my distance. I know it is the only thing that Jesus did against his will. It seems he didn't like it either.

I tend to enter the territory of the cross only when dragged there by the pain of my own sin. At these times I feel so bad about the mess I am in and feel so out of options that I may even fantasize or imagine a dramatic suicide. My method of choice is to crash through a concrete parapet on a significant bridge and drop, in terrifying finality, to the icy water below. Sometimes just simple physics brings me back to my senses. I realize that even at high speed my vehicle would not break through most concrete median barriers. I am then left with the humbling realization that my solution is not only immature, it is overkill. Something has to die, yes. It doesn't have to be my whole package (body, soul, and vehicle); it just has to be the part of me that is unpleasantly surfacing: my pride, control, or impatience. So in that moment, I often choose to follow Jesus to the place of death—the cross—and, usually reluctantly, surrender my beloved sin. In that sense I can relate to the cross as a multi-dimensional, time-spanning Christian place of transformational morbidity. It is the junkyard where I bring the destructive bits of my life that still cling to me and trade them for what Jesus always delivers to me: forgiveness and new life.

And so Christians hang a symbol of death around their necks. It's hard to imagine the new covenant being about death, yet to some extent it must be. The old in us must die—not just be put to sleep or pacified. Inasmuch as that is true, and it is, the cross is real and valid as a new-covenant symbol. Jesus resolutely set his face toward the city where his destiny was to be fulfilled—the city that held the cross. And having that resolute mindset is an important part of what the cross is about. But there was more to Jesus' story than the cross, or Good Friday. There was Easter Sunday, when he became alive. And so to fully symbolize what Christians believe needs more than a cross around our necks. The cross is the start, but life happens because of it, or around it, or on top of it.

The Celts placed a circle around the center of their cross. You can see these Celtic crosses in graveyards in Ireland and the world over. No one knows what the circle really was intended to mean, but it seems the Celts also recognized the bare cross was incomplete as a symbol for the new covenant. Perhaps the circle they added symbolized eternity, or life. It sat on top of, blended into, and wove through the cross and made it a more complete symbol of their faith: death for the purpose of new life.

Death always closes a door, and a cross thus symbolizes departing from the old. So the cross, as a symbol, takes one step out of the old covenant. It is only one step, though, because one or more deaths are not sustainable. The Celtic cross with its portrayal of death as well as life symbolizes completeness in the new covenant, something that can survive on its own. Into that we can symbolically move with both feet.

Saints

The accomplishments of the Irish indicate that their spiritual innovations had substance. As an example of the scope of their influence, consider St. Comgall, a contemporary of St. Brendan, who established the Abbey at Bangor in the mid sixth century. Annals give dates for the establishment between AD 552 and 559. A few decades later, St. Columbanus came to Bangor as a disciple and friend of Comgall and left, in 589, with his twelve companions to wander throughout Gaul and Italy, establishing many monasteries throughout that region. Those monasteries would become incubators of saints and apostles, sending off men who carried the rule of Columbanus, together with the gospel, into France, Germany, Switzerland, and Italy. Margaret Stokes, who did a pilgrimage through France in search of vestiges of the Irish saints, lists sixty-three such apostles from one monastery alone.[6] Bangor was sacked by the Norse in the ninth century, but later, in the Middle Ages, it would rekindle its spiritual flame and return to influence coming to be known in that time as the "Light of the World."

Men such as Comgall were called saints. The term could be interpreted as spiritual heavyweights. Adamnan documents the life of one of those saints, Columcille. The writing is perhaps more hagiography than biography, but even if it's only half true, Columcille was a spiritual heavyweight—someone to be reckoned with. He brought favor and healing with him and made short work of those who opposed him. He is said to have regularly confounded the local druids. He is also typically Irish in that one of his recorded miracles consists of bringing a sense of extreme serenity and bliss to his brothers as they commute home from work. One of his brothers described it by saying:

> I perceive the fragrance of such a wonderful odour, just as if all the flowers on earth were gathered together into one place; I feel also a glow of heat within me, not at all painful, but most pleasing, and a certain unusual and inexpressible joy poured into my heart, which on a sudden so refreshes and gladdens me, that I forget grief and weariness of every kind. Even the load, however heavy, which I carry on my back, is in some mysterious way so much lightened, from this place all the way to the monastery, that I do not seem to have any weight to bear.[7]

There are many other of these saints: St. Fursa, St. Brendan, St. Brigid, St. Killian, St. Ciàran (who founded the well-known monastery at Clonmacnoise), and there are still many more lesser saints of whom we know only their names and the areas they influenced. For a few centuries these men and women populated Ireland, wandered and settled in Europe, established monasteries, served as abbots and abbesses, and left their influence. Most lived and died in the favor of God and men; some obtained the martyrdom they sought. In our day, their number and stature would be impressive. In their time. it was even more so.

Wandering

We, today, rarely use the word *wandering* in a positive sense. People wander aimlessly or wander from their faith; wheels wander out of alignment. Yet the Irish viewed wandering as an undeniably positive characteristic and rediscovered themselves in their wandering. I say rediscovered because the Irish were wanderers from the beginning. One of the earliest Irish stories is the tale of the voyage of Bran who, while wandering near his home on a quest for the Other World, received a vision. An angelic messenger describes a land of promise to Bran that prompts him to leave his home and make an extended voyage across the sea in search of it. The land of promise is described to Bran as the Land of Women and the Land of Joy. With that description Bran apparently has no trouble gathering an ensemble and sets off the next day with a company of men. In true Irish fashion, the ocean he sets out on is not as substantial as we might expect. A mythical figure they meet reveals that the ocean actually is a flowery plain. After that encounter and some further sailing, the crew encounters the land of promise. Bran and his crew stay at both places of perfection and beauty. But, after a year or so, Bran feels compelled to return. He travels back across the sea to find that ages of time have passed in his hometown. People there don't recognize him anymore. They are unable to communicate with him. He and his crew, save one who tries to stay, and in the process turns to ashes, return to their ships and remain perpetual ocean travelers.

This myth reveals the Irish penchant for travel, particularly travel that has the goals of spirituality and promise. That penchant continues after the Irish conversion. The early Irish Christians embarked on a unique kind of travel that emphasized wandering. Nora Chadwick says that the love of wandering is one of the most striking and original features of Irish Christianity. She also says that love of wandering was something that was true in both the literal and figurative sense.[8] They wandered not from boredom, but out of a sense of calling. They wandered, as noted in chapter 5, to find the place of their resurrection, but wandering was also about deliberate uncertainty. In wandering, your journey was arranged in a way that encouraged the surroundings and events to come upon you as something new. Irish wanderers would head out singly or in small bands or in groups of twelve. They generally followed no fixed plan. St. Columba left Ireland for Britain to wander for Christ. This wandering was the impetus behind the Irish scattering into Europe. They became *peregrini,* or wanderers, who traveled great distances and entered new territory to find the place of their own. Some were bishops before leaving Ireland and would remain without a diocese or fixed territory in their new land. Some would be raised to bishops by their peers in their newfound country. The strolling bishops, as they were also called, were welcomed by kings and by the people they served, but not always by the local religious leaders, who are noted to have considered their teaching of Christianity too unfettered.[9]

Many Irish saints went further than *peregrini* and chose the life of *perigrinatio*: exiles for Christ. They exiled themselves from their homelands in an ascetic expression of love for Christ. Some expressed their spirituality by traveling to isolated places like the craggy pyramids of rock that project from the North Atlantic south of the Kerry coast: the Skellig Rocks. They lie twelve kilometers from the closest point of Irish coastline and today that journey takes just twenty minutes. In the days before powerboats, the Irish who populated this rock would have sailed or rowed out. In the early part of the last century, when the experience of travel was similar to what it would have been like for those *peregrenatio*, George Bernard Shaw went to the Skellig Rocks. He wrote this the next day, on September 18, 1910, to a friend:

Yesterday I left the Kerry coast in an open boat, 33 feet long, propelled by ten men on five oars. These men started on 49 strokes a minute, a rate which I did not believe they could keep up for five minutes. They kept it without slackening half a second for two hours, at the end of which they landed me on the most fantastic and impossible rock in the world: Skellig Michael, or the Great Skellig, where in south west gales the spray knocks stones out of the lighthouse keeper's house, 160 feet above calm sea level. There is a little Skellig covered with gannets—white with them (and their guano)—covered with screaming crowds of them. The Bass rock is a mere lump in comparison: both the Skelligs are pinnacled, crocketed, spired, arched, caverned, minaretted; and these gothic extravagances are not curiosities of the islands: they are the islands: there is nothing else.[10]

Irish monks inhabited Skellig Michael for hundreds of years—until (and in some sense after) the Norse invasions. They built winding stone staircases on it to help them manage the long hike from shore to crest. The stone stairs look as though they were inlaid in the moss that now grows in the sheltered, steep valley. As the last stair passes behind you, at the crest of the crag, a cluster of stony beehive-shaped huts comes into view. This is the village the monks inhabited for centuries. The stones are dry stacked and the huts, to an untrained eye, look prone to leaking, but they are surprisingly watertight. Standing next to one of those huts provides a palpable sense of isolation. Other than the smaller Skellig, which is nearby, all you can see from the monastery area is the open and unencumbered Atlantic Ocean. The environment seems to amplify the power of the wind and sea. The monks likely ate gannet and got most of their other food from the sea. Professor John Macquarrie said of the Christian Celts in general: "The Celt was very much a God-intoxicated man whose life was embraced on all sides by the divine Being."[11] This must certainly have been true of those who lived on Skellig Michael.

There is something clearly unique in the Irish wandering. While Patrick had a defined purpose and goal in his travels, which was to bring many into the kingdom, the later Irish seemed motivated as much by a desire to wander and follow their hearts. The missionary results that later Irish produced were similar to Patrick's except they seemed to come mostly as a byproduct. The Celts always valued their choice and their freedom to exercise it. It's no coincidence that the apostle Paul's letter to the Galatians (Celts) emphasized the freedom that they had been given and scolded them for abandoning it. Freedom is close to the Irish heart, and that sense of freedom invaded all of the Celtic Christians' actions. The Irish saints were well known for evangelizing much of the European continent after the fall of the Roman Empire, but it is worth noting that their motivation for evangelism appeared far from a guilt-driven need to make converts. Rather, they were motivated by the desire to explore their freedom and enhance the experience of the life they received. The Irish were holy and they traveled. That combination produced influence. They were not those who welcomed a task defined solely as a burden—they had had their fill of that. The Irish reconceived evangelism as a task that came deep from within the heart of the giver and had, as an unexpected result, the influence of the heart of the receiver.

Wandering points us to the reality that, to some extent, the Irish adopted what we earlier defined as the essential objective of spiritual life—to obtain as much of that life as possible. Their primary objective was obtaining life and their goal (wandering) was designed to achieve that higher objective. Both seem, to me, abstract and unproductive. A mission agency would have difficulty raising funds by advertising those goals and objectives. Yet funding of this type of phenomenon apparently makes sense, because the Irish actions ended up producing astounding results on many practical and measurable levels. Why? The Irish show us that inasmuch as their actions appeared impractical on the surface, at a deep level they were effective because they were consistent with the primary feature of our age—the new covenant. There is a reality that those who truly love, desire, and worship Jesus cannot help but produce good. If we find their actions odd, it is likely because our mindset is focused on understanding and managing the apparent links between cause and effect while having little concern about how our attitudes or actions mesh with the new covenant.

Adventure

We have seen how the gospel unearthed the Irish character and magnified it—made it new. They found themselves rediscovering their inherently Irish traits—traits that made them Celtic, and made them successful in the past. Their actions, post gospel, not only confirm our understanding of their past—they were the subjects of religious abuse—but they also describe the way toward newness for those of us freed from religious affectations. We noted earlier that the early Celts—those before the Roman Empire—were the dominant European culture. For two centuries they populated an area stretching from Ireland to Galatia. Celtic scholar Myles Dillon notes, "This rapid expansion over an enormous area implies great fecundity and a great spirit of adventure."[12] This expansion indicates the true nature of the Celts. They had a spirit of adventure and, to use an old but valuable term, fecundity. Six hundred years later, their advances had been curtailed. They had been pushed back to the remote corners of the world—the island of Ireland and parts of Scotland. Their armies had been dominated by the Roman military. But the gospel that took root in those remote parts rejuvenated their spirit of fecundity and adventure. It reawakened the Irish at a core level. Not surprisingly, when they were so awakened, the Irish rapidly expanded over almost the same territory—this time for the gospel.

It sounds too good to be true. Yes, the gospel truly speaks of surrender. Yes, Jesus truly spoke of the narrow road into the kingdom. Yes, sin truly kills its participants. Yet apparently one more primary truth applies to our age. One that is also almost too good to be true. We are fearfully and wonderfully made and our

Maker has a strong desire for us to rediscover that reality. He has tilted the spiritual landscape so that the gospel, once received, can obliterate much of what religion considers important. The result is to make you free to be more like you—for the primary reason that your soul would fully connect to the soul at the heart of the universe.

Everything has been said before, but since nobody listens we have to keep going back and beginning all over again.

—Andre Gide

CHAPTER 8

Rejuvenating Ancient Traits

WE CONSIDERED HOW the gospel rejuvenated ancient Celtic traits. One of those traits was an attraction to adventure. It was a hallmark of their Iron-Age culture—as evidenced by the way they dominated most of Europe. But by the time of Patrick in the fifth century, their adventuresome ways were barely evident. As a people, they had been corralled into a small territory. The territories they had surrendered to the Romans in Gaul, Galatia, and elsewhere had become provinces and lost much of their Celtic cultural flavor. Their glory days were gone; their sense of identity was waning. Even in Ireland, where the influence of Romans was minimal, many of the Celtic cultural distinctives related to what they did not do. It was a time that could have been the beginning of the end for the Celts. In many ways it was a post-Celtic period. Yet something about the gospel was so entirely new that it rekindled something ancient in this post-Celtic society. The gospel renewed something within their culture and they were again motivated to expand across Europe and spread their influence. They became new in a way that remembered the best from their past. What was astounding about the ancient Irish result was how the particular trait God resurrected among the Irish, a spirit of adventure, was so well suited for their circumstance.

Positive Inertia

Rejuvenating an ancient cultural trait is certainly worthwhile—something with inherent value. Who wouldn't want something positive from their ancient past rekindled? To me, it has incredible appeal.

Often all that gets carried forward from past generations are negative traits and a sense of negative generational inertia. Wouldn't it be great to participate in the opposite kind of inertia with positive effects and blessings being brought forward? What would it take to get to that point?

In this chapter I will suggest a couple things are helpful to reach that point: terminating old habits and mindsets, and solidifying our knowledge of new-covenant truth.

Terminate Old Habits

Though it sounds redundant, we must turn from the old to adopt the new. It's worth discussing this step—which often seems too basic to merit discussion—because we cling to old habits. We might pay lip service to things new and profess to embrace them, but when they arrive, we naturally return to the old. Whether it's a new business strategy, a new community, a new job, a new country, new math, new economics, a new phase in life, or any other form of newness, they are all unknown, undefined, and have little precedent. For these reasons, newness is full of turmoil. Spiritual newness inhabits the most tumultuous category of newness because it threatens some of our most treasured reserves of sameness. Spiritual newness tampers with our security blankets and our tradition-bound pacifiers—the unchanging bedrock of our lives. Accepting spiritual newness often doesn't happen without a significant amount of turmoil associated with turning from the old.

The turmoil is worthwhile if it moves us forward. I recall a time when I was sitting in church, the pastor was speaking, and my mind wandered, in this case to my grades in the subjects of life. They were subjects like

- Business owner
- Husband
- Father
- Writer
- Church member
- Missions supporter

It seemed clear that the grade I was achieving in all those subjects was below average: a D or maybe even an F. That conclusion didn't feel exaggerated or self-generated to illicit pity. Rather it seemed borne out of a moment of clarity. I recognized that, by normal standards of measurement, my performance was behind the curve and below the median in all those subjects. It seemed to me the grades were on 4 x 6 cards floating in front of me. I couldn't deny them; doing something immediate like giving them to Jesus seemed oddly impossible or inappropriate. It seemed I just had to face them. After a while I realized how hard it was for someone used to getting As as a kid in school to deal with so many Fs. It was out of sync with my reality—upside down. I thought of the verse I had been meditating on: "Blessed are the poor in spirit for theirs is the kingdom of heaven." That is an entirely upside-down passage of Scripture, and through it I heard God say, "You have to close the door to the old."

I had been studying and thinking about the new covenant for almost ten years at that point. It had caused joy, turmoil, curiosity, and hope in my life. I knew it was real and knew it represented what Jesus was about, yet with that statement I recognized I was still quite invested in an old way of living. And that old way was not working for me anymore. What was also clearly not working was sitting on the fence between the old and the new. So the time seemed appropriate to make a decision away from the old and toward the new. And I felt some deep inner calm at the prospect of doing that. I didn't really know what old things I would close the door to, but I suspected they were going to include things such as

- performing,
- keeping time,
- following the rules,
- making it,
- being "good,"
- focusing on what others think,
- controlling others.

I didn't know it then, but that decision was the seed of change in my life—a change to a new location, a better job, a more suitable church, a revived outlook, and a renewed passion for God. At that moment in church, I did not know what my future held; I only knew I wanted no more of the old. For the rest of that day, and other days after it, I just continued to meditate on what I consider the anchor chapter of the new covenant—the beatitudes in Matthew 5: "Blessed are the poor in spirit [those at the end of their ropes]," for theirs is the kingdom of heaven (verse 3). As I pondered that, I was able to slowly release my grip on my old way of doing things.

It was as though choosing to turn from the old way was like throwing out a collection of spiritual idols. A collection I didn't even know I had. The ancient Israelites responded to the prophet Samuel's pleas to follow the Lord with all their hearts by "putting away their Baals and Ashtoreths, and serving the LORD only."[1] It seems that throughout history, our natural tendency is to collect beliefs, religious idols, and safeguards. We seem to naturally want to hedge our bets and maximize our odds. We start figuring the angles and think the more theologies, the more idols, we have the better. No matter that they contradict each other. We use the idol we need when appropriate and put it back on the shelf when not. It's the same today with the new covenant. We probably have intuitively recognized its essence—Jesus—but we have also diluted it by adding other old (but familiar) pieces to it when we feel they are necessary. We add laws when we want to control, we stress historical precedent when we are fearful of outcomes, we create a standard mode of operating because we don't trust the Spirit of God to do his work. Clinging to those idols has an appearance of logic or minimized risk, but in reality it minimizes the effect of what's real—the new covenant.

It's in that context that Jesus, without intending disrespect toward parents, said to the follower who was concerned about his father's funeral, "...let the dead bury their own dead."[2] He also told his disciples to hate their fathers and mothers.[3] These are extreme statements, and Jesus never seemed to shy away from using a provocative phrase to emphasize the important features of his message. In this case, familial loyalty, though good and honorable, tends to perpetuate the old and cannot stand in the way.

This has more than theoretical importance. Parents invest time and effort in their kids, and every parent builds expectations. In our pluralistic and individualistic world the nature of those expectations varies widely, but most children figure out what they are and comply with them—some immediately and some after a period of rebellion. Likely because parents have charge of their kids in the most formative years of their lives, most kids eventually validate the German proverb that says, the apple doesn't fall far from the stem. So Jesus, whose goal is to change the world, has to point to something larger than the critical need to honor parents—he points to the need to honor the truth, and he does so in a way that recognizes the first step at least may feel culturally awkward.

At some point a decision is required from every follower of Jesus—to follow him into the territory of the new that he opens. This requires leaving the old territory. It's not a step of rebellion or a step borne out of anger. It's primarily a step of surrender and obedience.

Anchor Points

The turning from the old is a milestone event. It releases grace to face the new territory, and once we turn from the old we want to keep from turning back toward it. In order to do that, we need to remind ourselves of what is true.

There are many features of the new covenant we can ponder, meditate on, and assemble in defense against the old or "the religious" who oppose it. Most of these new perspectives require an ongoing adjustment of mindset. If, like me, you come from a religious background and want to return to the God of the new covenant, you may require defenses against the old perspectives.

In the old covenant the anchor chapters are Deuteronomy 28–30. They outline the rules of that covenant, which appear relatively simple: obey God and be blessed; disobey and be cursed. The prophets, who later challenged Israel, exhaustively elaborated on these anchor chapters: If you want to get blessed—if you want to live in houses others have built—obey. If you want curses—if you want to plant vineyards and have someone else eat the fruit—disobey. The overarching theme was God stands by his covenant promises and you can rely on that.

In the new covenant God has a new promise, and a primary feature of the covenant is its wordlessness. That makes enough of a statement on its own, but the questions remain: What written words can we rely on? What are the anchor points for our covenant? What do we meditate on to fortify ourselves? How do we fix our minds on truth?

The New Testament

If you've had any previous contact with church, you may have spent time reading and considering the Bible and the New Testament. You will get the most value considering it from a new-covenant perspective. With the right perspective, the New Testament will lead us further into new-covenant truth—it contains the anchor chapters and the written words we need. With the wrong perspective, it can seem full of landmines. It often has seemed full of landmines to me.

One landmine-laden perspective is to view the Bible, as I have in the past and as I've noticed many people do, as a collection of chapters and verses—like a database. When you study a topic of concern with this perspective, your job is to find all the verses you can on that topic, assemble them, compare them, and come to a conclusion. You try to consider each verse without bias and apply equal weight to each word. You consider each text having the same authority to speak to you, as you would data points. This perspective led to problems for me because data points don't capture the significance of timing and audience. The Bible is not a level book. It says of itself that much of what is written within it pales in comparison to what is revealed in Jesus. As we said earlier, an important feature of our age is to recognize which covenant is operational. The database approach often neglects this important aspect.

Another perspective, one that I grew up with, views verses and chapters in the Bible as building in intensity or authority over the years until they climax in significance—with Jesus. When Jesus arrives and walks on the earth, his words are considered heavily weighted data. They are printed in red and treated with extra value. This perspective has a lot of merit, but after Jesus' resurrection and ascension, the words spoken on his behalf are no longer in red. With this perspective comes a hint or suggestion that authority and intensity decrease in the years following Jesus' physical presence on earth. It seems like periods of time close to when Jesus walked the earth have more importance than those far away. Those who hold to this perspective, for example, might place a high value on the study of the early church. For all its value, this perspective is not a fully new-covenant perspective because of the way it considers authority and significance trailing off.

There are many ways of considering the Bible. I bring up the previous simple perspectives only as background to this question: How can we view the words of the Bible from a new covenant perspective? If you come from a religious background, I believe only a new-covenant perspective will remove the apparent landmines associated with Bible study. It will help make sense of trivial matters and profound. In the realm of trivial, the new covenant helps explain why the New Testament is much shorter than the Old. If Jesus is the Word of God to us and we have his law written on our hearts, then that moderates our real need for voluminous scripture. I am thankful for every word we have. We need the primary markers, the insight, the teaching, and the examples, but apparently we don't need a lot more; and what we do need, we can get directly.

The way the books written after Jesus were confirmed as authoritative also makes new-covenant sense. People decided which books belonged and which ones did not, unlike some of the old covenant in which God himself wrote things in stone. In the New Testament words obtain their authority because they contain some recognizable truth and because people (the church) recognized them as having power. The process of assembling the inspired Word of God was the work of people. Various church synods and individuals wrestled over which writings were suitable for the Bible. They developed criteria of authenticity and then set about evaluating the books that existed. Many books were already recognized as inspired by the masses and some were argued over at length by scholars. The point is that the New Testament is authoritative, and a large part of its authority is derived from those whom God has given real authority in our age—the people with the law written on their hearts.

The New Testament starts by revealing the person on which the covenant revolves—Jesus. The first four books describe his life and their repetitive emphasis is clear. This book, the Bible, only makes sense because of this person, Jesus. The words of the New Testament are important in that they communicate the higher principle of the new covenant—the true Word—Jesus.

> The one use of the Bible is to make us look at Jesus, that through Him we might know His Father and our Father, His God and our

God. Till we thus know Him, let us hold the Bible dear as the moon of our darkness, by which we travel toward the east; not dear as the sun whence her light cometh, and towards which we haste, that, walking in the sun himself, we may no more need the mirror that reflected his absent brightness...
—George Macdonald (1824–1905), *The Higher Faith*

After starting with Jesus, the New Testament develops consistently with a new-covenant mindset. Consider the apostle Paul—who wrote most of the remaining books. Without a new-covenant framework, his influence in the Bible seems all out of proportion. Years ago, I was scanning through the library. I saw a book titled *The Christian Problem* by Stuart Rosenberg and opened it because I suspected it would provide some suitable arguments I could satisfactorily dissect. Reading it, however, I discovered well-considered "problems" with Christian thought for which I had no immediate answer. I closed the book and walked home—surprisingly wounded in my silent theological sparring and slightly disturbed.

One objection Rosenberg raised that I did not resolve without a new-covenant perspective was the issue of Paul's influence. Rosenberg said the gospel was more the product of Paul's fertile mind than it was the result of the teachings of Jesus. Paul took the revolutionary teachings of Jesus and wrapped his own ideas about freedom, grace, and sin around them to produce what we now call Christianity. He was illegitimate, the author argued, because he never spent any physical time with the faith's real founder. He was one of those dominant personalities who hijacks a group of people and takes them in the direction he desires.

This problematic view of Paul is real for many biblical mindsets. But the new covenant recognizes that the gospel was not winding down after Jesus walked the earth—it had just begun. Paul had seen no less of Jesus than the Twelve. In fact he'd seen more. He'd seen the eternal, resurrected, glorified Jesus—with no knowledge of Jesus' bodily presence to limit his perception. Paul had every right to define the gospel of the new covenant in terms the Greeks would understand. He, in fact, was the first of many messengers of the new covenant. It was no coincidence that this first messenger was not of the Twelve. That would've made his position historically static. People would've said, "He did those great things because he lived and ate with Jesus." No—his distance from the physical Jesus made Paul, in many respects, the first new-covenant messenger.

Paul took the first new-covenant risk. He reworded the gospel to suit his hearers. He didn't change any of the substance, but reached down into the core to pull up the very aspect of the gospel that would woo the hearts of the Gentiles. Jesus didn't talk a lot about grace and peace, he lived it. Paul talked about the grace and truth the risen Jesus had ministered to him and so expounded on the gospel.

Why is it that Jesus rarely explained himself? Why did he leave it to Paul? Because, as a man—in particular a Hebrew man, speaking to Hebrew audiences—Jesus couldn't possibly have explained himself adequately. He just did what he came to do and he did it perfectly. Paul did the explaining of Jesus to the Greek mind. Patrick did a pretty good job of explaining Jesus to the Irish, and there are many explanations left unspoken out there. Explanations for you and me to make to the audience we are drawn to.

Jesus' life, when taken to the full extent of its scope, envelopes every truth of God. The foundational aspect of his work was his sacrificial death for our life. But that reality, and that life, can be outworked in so many ways and revealed in so many cultures that it, in fact, has no bounds. So in answer to Stuart Rosenberg, Paul had as much right as we do to define Jesus and hijack the gospel, for those who feel culturally separated from him today. Those who have followed Paul's daring example and have not fallen prey to believing that they are God rather than his messengers have seen the same results as he did. In that sense, when I read St. Patrick's *Confession,* I at once feel as though I am reading Paul. He seems astounded at how God uses him, talks often of grace, and influences thousands.

The goal of the new covenant is not simply to find new ways to understand the Bible, even though it does give me those. I take comfort when I read a verse like Psalm 25:10: "All the ways of the LORD are loving and faithful toward those who keep the demands of his covenant." I think to myself, "I qualify for that blessing because God's covenant for this age is to pour his Spirit on all flesh (which includes me) and because I rely on Jesus, the covenant inaugurator." The Old Testament is superseded, but not devoid of meaning. I read many old-covenant passages through the lens of 2 Corinthians 1:20: "For no matter how many promises God has made, they are 'Yes' in Christ." It's a fantastically positive statement of fulfillment.

I used to avoid Bible passages that I now love because I now understand their new-covenant meaning. Of course, there are still many things I do not understand. Like the Irish, I am glad God is mysterious, and just because I don't understand something does not make it untrue. I put the mysterious issues on the shelf and sometimes after a year or two, they are less of a mystery—sometimes their meaning is clear. The new covenant does not primarily give us the ability and tools to systematize a new theology. Quite the contrary. It is okay to have thoughts, concepts, ideas, and verses on the shelf. What's comforting is that the questions have a context.

The Bounds

When we start cracking open the new covenant, we get into heady territory and it's easy to see why protective leaders want to keep this explosive material somewhat contained. From the Celts we learned that newness on its own presents a huge territory—one too big to navigate. Shape-shifting and other manifestations of unbounded newness became the bane of their existence. Newness is a can of worms. When anyone opens the door to radical newness he or she usually steps into a short-lived situation. Newness is a paradigm that, once established, is not easily contained. The pioneer who leads his followers from tradition-bound sameness into the realm of newness can easily become last week's news—stranded in obsolescence and overtaken by the next new thing from the next new leader. And where does that leave the pioneer's followers? They've got neither their tradition nor their beloved leader. Once you succumb to the great appeal of Jesus' newness and cut your ties to your traditional past, what will prevent you from being overtaken by the next super-jesus—one who will unexpectedly walk through the door you've opened, claim to be newer, and appear smarter, but who will likely be less caring and less appealing?

A while ago, I opened the newspaper to read about a certain Russian named Piotr Kuznetsov, who left his architectural profession to set up a spiritual community in the Russian countryside. People came to his village in droves and enjoyed the community and the prayer. One day, they disappeared. At the time the article was written, they were holed up in an elaborate, underground cave, where they had been for months. They were awaiting the apocalypse, which Mr. Kuznetsov predicted would occur in May of 2008. When his prediction failed, Mr. Kuznetsov is said to have repeatedly hit himself on the head with a log. He turned out to be another prophet with a message that served primarily to lead people astray.

To settle our minds, we need the new-covenant bounds. Where are the limits? We saw how it started, but how does it end? Bounds are worth considering before plunging into the ocean of newness. Thankfully, Jesus thought of them in advance. He promised, as the Good Shepherd, to always care for us and we know not to look for another prophet to usher in the next age because Jesus himself told us when the age would end—with his return. We know that Jesus won't be superseded because he did not leave newness unbounded. He told us what to look for and how he would return. Each covenant has its messenger. Jesus put a fence around the new covenant on both sides. He initiated it with the Last Supper and spoke of the times at the end of the new-covenant age.

Have you encountered humanist admirers of Jesus? Maybe you are one yourself. These are people who find little that is appealing in the confines of a church building, but find the historical person of Jesus incredibly compelling. They find him compassionate, just, politically shrewd, and amazingly effective at transforming history. In my experience, these admirers usually are disturbed and confused about his troublesome talk about the end of the age. Why was that necessary? Could he not have changed the world without all that end-time prognostication? Especially since little of it seems to have yet occurred. The new covenant provides an answer to this concern because discussion of the end of the age is necessary for someone whose job it is to open the door to something radically new. Jesus knew that one of his main tasks was to confirm he was the last "new." He is the Alpha and Omega and by speaking of the end of the age—as well as its beginning—he did what he needed to do to effectively close the door on those who would claim to supersede him. He bounded the territory, so we can safely explore it.

The new covenant is, for our understanding, the last covenant. God necessarily saved the most potent covenant for the last. With a name like the new covenant, could it be any other way? The Bible describes no other covenant. Even when the age is ending, as in the Revelation description of the opening of the seals, the authority for the actions is described in new-covenant terminology. The Lamb who was slain has the authority to break the seals.

After our age ends, there is "what is to come." Much of the fulfilled promises that God made—including full realization of the new covenant when truly "all will know me from the least to the greatest," gathering Israel back to their own land so they will live in the land of Jacob forever, putting his sanctuary among them—falls under what prophets alternately call the new covenant or the everlasting covenant. The everlasting covenant is not separate from the new covenant, but outside the scope of this discussion.

The Essence

The basis of the new covenant is God turning his heart toward his children and going to great lengths to do so. The root of a new-covenant mindset is recognizing God's heart for us—his desire to know us and be in relationship with us. To live fully in that reality, everything we read and do must get filtered through that mindset. Remember, God wiped the previous slate clean in order to get here. Anything we understand that is contrary to the message of heart connection is either misinformed or a deception. That's why stories like the prodigal son in the Bible are so pivotal. When Jesus ranted at the Pharisees and called them whitewashed tombs, some think he was getting angry at sin. More to the point, he was using razor-sharp words because he knew those kinds of words were necessary to pierce their religious armor. The words were evidence of his goal for them—relationship. It was an effective strategy and it worked. Some, like Nicodemus, followed.

When we see someone steeped in a destructive life pattern, a new-covenant mindset yearns to see a restored relationship. An old-covenant mindset reacts out of anger, thoughts of violation of law, and judgment.

Adventure

We started this chapter with a desire to connect with positive inertia. We waded through the safeguards and theology to get what the Irish had, which was the ability to dig into their past and rekindle the core values—the spark within their background—and express that in a new way. The theology is really about removing roadblocks so the connection can happen. The Father-son, or Father-daughter, connection is the engine that does the work.

The Irish started with a spirit of adventure and God resurrected it. A spirit of adventure is a strikingly fitting characteristic for those being given the gift of something new. Adventure helps engage the gift of newness and conquer the fear behind it.

I think not only the warlike Irish need their spirit of adventure rekindled, it's something required of any who pursue newness. To love newness is to love adventure. To have newness rekindled is to have your spirit of adventure rekindled. You have to love adventure to long for newness. You need to have a desire to leave your comfortable village and wander off into the wide open world. You have to love adventure to cast off your old druidic leaders based on a hope that the new leaders will have something better to offer.

Thank God Patrick chose to embrace the newness he was dealt. We too have a choice. We live in an age of golden opportunity; it's our privilege to participate in it. I suspect all of heaven watches us with a sense of awe to see how much of the reality of this new-covenant age we participate in. Our leader, Jesus, has said he will recognize every effort we make, surprisingly ignore every mistake we make, and acknowledge every risk we take for his kingdom. In some sense we can't lose. In the language of financial markets, our risks are hedged. Why not risk?

There is nothing more difficult to take in hand, more perilous to conduct, or more uncertain in its success, than to take a lead in the introduction of a new order of things, because the innovator has for enemies all those who have done well under the old conditions, and lukewarm defenders in those who may do well under the new. This coolness arises partly from fear…and partly from the incredulity of men, who do not readily believe in new things until they have had a long experience of them.

—Nicolo Machiavelli, *The Prince*

CHAPTER 9

THE NEXT STEP

A LIFELONG SURFER once told me that waves are the heartbeat of the ocean. The new covenant is like God's heartbeat made audible for us. Words don't serve very well in describing something like that. Clearly, most words we use to describe the new covenant will be insufficient. But what can we say to describe the next steps we take to pursue this heartbeat?

If there are steps, the New Testament often chooses to lay them out in stories and word pictures. For example, Jesus said trying to blend the old with the new was as nonsensical as putting a patch of new cloth on an old garment.[1] The new patch will shrink and pull apart the tear, leaving the garment in a worse condition. New things act on their surroundings in significant and irrestrainable ways. In the story Jesus stated that what he came to bring had yet to go through its cycle of effect on society. It needed to act on its environment and it would be irrestrainable. It would burst out of structures that tried, in an old-fashioned way, to contain it. That cycle of effect is not yet over and the bursting is still occurring. Trying to restrain it with parts of the old is a nonstarter for those who want to live in sync with the reality of our age.

Luke strategically places the story of a curious man walking with two disciples to Emmaus at the end of his gospel. It is the last impression he wants to leave with his readers as they consider Jesus. The disciples walked and talked on the road with this man they did not recognize. Yet their hearts were burning. They learned a great deal from the man they traveled with and when they invited him to stay longer, he did. They recognized him fully when he broke bread (a reference to the new covenant) for who he was—Jesus. Then he vanished.

That *Twilight Zone* type of story encapsulates so many aspects of the new-covenant journey. Jesus and the new covenant is the key to understanding God in this age. But understanding, in itself, is not the goal. When the travelers understood who Jesus was, the person they understood vanished. The goal of the new-covenant journey is more than understanding, it is relationship; there is an element of mystery. The story is both profound and a little bit frustrating at the same time. How do you write a manual based on that? If there was a manual it would say this is something that must be discovered. It's new because it's not about a system, it's about a heart beating for another heart. It's about a Father's longing for his children and turning his heart toward them.

Do the Celts really show us the way to discover the new covenant? There are indicators that what the Celts experienced was exceptional and instructional. There is the pragmatic argument. What the Celts did worked. The Celtic transformation is enviable no matter what caused it. That the gospel was behind the transformation is encouraging for Christians. That we can learn from them seems obvious.

Patrick was saved without human agency. He met God amongst his pagan "hosts" and in the midst of sheep. He had a direct encounter with heaven that was not mediated through another human being. In this way, Patrick met God just like Jeremiah prophesied: "no longer will a man teach his neighbor, for they will all know me."[2] He met God like another pioneer and apostle of the new covenant, Paul. Paul met God on the road to Damascus in a blaze of blinding light. His encounter was not mediated, or even comprehended, by those who were with him at the time. Paul had to sit in a blinded stupor for days and then in the desert for a few years to make sense of his encounter with God and to rearrange his theology. Both Patrick's and Paul's encounters with Jesus signify something apostolic, something that communicates and foreshadows a delivery of truth from heaven to earth.

Patrick's story has survived throughout centuries, making the case for providence. We know the mythical Patrick, but we also can read documents from his own hand. This is astounding considering that almost fifteen hundred years have passed. The survival stands as providential evidence his story was meant to be preserved. Likewise, the Celtic flavor of the gospel was not kept contained, but rather was allowed to be seeded across Europe. It was not defined as a heresy or squashed. Its reputation was retained and it was allowed to blossom and reproduce. If you believe in God's ability to direct history, then this is an experiment that was meant to have effect and meant to be considered.

The gospel always saves people from a problem. Perhaps the most instructional element from the Irish story is that the felt problem for the Irish was not "How do I rid myself of guilt and sin?" Their problem was "How do I connect with the beauty and perfection I desire?" They recognized that beauty was out there and was primarily spiritual. They recognized the power of words; they imagined a word of truth at the core of the universe; they longed for a connection to the spirit world. The new covenant provides for all those things and provides the power to battle against the failure of previous attempts, which were marred with foolishness, sin, and deception.

Hopefully you can relate in some sense to the Irish experience and see how it leads to the reality of the new covenant and most importantly how it opens the door for more of an experience of it. The Irish started to step into new territory. God seemed intent on preserving that start and amplifying it. Our job is to take the next step.

We cannot repeat the Irish experience or pretend to be Celts. As we noted earlier, they may be your distant ancestors, but their golden age was a product of a certain historical context. Economies, politics, technology, and people create history. Those factors change

The Irish and the Blank Page

with time. Nora Chadwick eloquently describes how studying any period in history is like watching a freighter pass by the shore. It comes into view, fills up your field of vision, recedes from view, and then disappears—never to be seen again. The Celtic age of saints is a treasure from the past that we can marvel at and hopefully learn from in our own times but, sadly, one that has receded and will never return.[3] Not in the same way it was first experienced. The Irish towns, monasteries, and communities were overtaken and destroyed by Norse invaders. Even the monastic community on the Skellig Rocks was raided by Vikings in the ninth century, though it remained a habitation of monks until the twelfth century.

So if we want what the Irish had, we need to learn from them. The thing that awakened the productive passion they were privileged to experience over fifteen hundred years ago was their fortuitous connection with the new covenant. This connection was facilitated by their need. They were desperate for freedom and for release from the restrictive set of circumstances in which they found themselves. After they connected with the new covenant, they were left undisturbed by those enmeshed in traditional beliefs. They were left to set their own gospel path. They were free to experiment with the core of the gospel, and they produced surprising and appealing results.

Their historical experiment was fantastic, but what does it have to say to those of us who want to participate in the new covenant today?

Intentionality

For us to experience what the Celts experienced of the new covenant will take intentionality. It won't come by passive consent. Part of the reason for this is because of the different way we receive wrath and grace. This may surprise you. When you live in the old covenant and believe you are the object of wrath, your environment may not be enjoyable, but it has some consistency and provides some meaning. It may consistently deliver negative feelings, but the consistent delivery makes you feel worth scolding and you certainly don't feel ignored. Wrath provides an odd context. When someone is continually scolded, at some point the scolding becomes a discordant background music to his or her life. When that scolding, or wrath, is removed there can be a void, a meaninglessness, a lack of purpose. Where did the noise go? Our world is full of that meaninglessness. But the new covenant has removed God's wrath and created that space. When artists, theologians, or prophets tell us that God's wrath is removed, after the euphoria, a disconcerting void and resulting lack of identity can result. That void is really an opportunity to seek the new.

But many of us have become so used to the passive posture associated with receiving wrath. Because God, in the new covenant, treats us like adults, the passive posture no longer fits. We need to actively seek God's love and grace. We need to listen for his voice. Love and grace are not in limited supply or scarce, but we need to choose to believe in them and choose to experience them. So, it may seem odd, but to live in the new-covenant age we need to be active and intentional. The dreams and visions of the new covenant are for those who anticipate them—like Virgil the Geometer, Abbot of Aghaboe in Ireland, who voluntarily exiled himself from Ireland "for the love of Christ" and set out intentionally to express his passion for God.[4] To be otherwise, to be passive, is to slip back in the environment of (fabricated) wrath and/or endure meaninglessness.

God Without an Agenda

North American culture, like the precontact Irish culture, is a culture that was once more than it currently is. It's looking for something to rekindle the past fire and rejuvenate past strengths. We're looking for something that will reveal our identity. Our culture, like theirs, also seems lost in a sea of control. The things that control us, of course, are different from the superstitions and fears that controlled the Celts. They were drawn to beauty and perfection. They were vulnerable to those who would interpret the unknown things of the world—often to their disadvantage. We are drawn toward knowledge and are aware of the power of our choices. The forces that bombard us tempt us with the thing we crave (knowledge) and satiate our ability to choose. We are bathed in a sea of commercial influence, peddling, and manipulation. Every man-made object, whether the paint on the side of a bus or the arrangement of an interior space, seems designed to get us to do something, to buy something, to be safer, to pollute less, to think of poorer nations. The causes are often good, but the sum of the efforts to direct our thoughts and actions can be dehumanizing. In the end, we become either cynics who say no without thinking, or fools who choose, often against our better judgment, to say yes to the influencers. In many cases we've given up on beauty. The concepts of individual will and personal value have eroded.

Even in sacred places, like when we meet as the church, we are not so much fearfully and wonderfully made creatures who gather to join our souls in the worship of our Creator. We are, rather, holders of time, money, and/or influence that come together to be influenced by those with an agenda, even God's agenda. We come to hear the latest cause and to be influenced to effect change. We come to be influenced to join some group or another. It makes many of us want to run away to some place where people value the sense of mystery and take pleasure in things half said.

The Celtic experience speaks powerfully to those of us in a postmodern culture because it reveals a God who is willing to place his agenda on the sideline in order to know our hearts and to find his. God—as his new covenant describes him, and as the Celts understood him—was the Creator who delighted in them finding their own place within his creation: their place of resurrection. They wandered because they could. They doodled in their manuscripts because they felt that leaving a little of their own identity in the pages of Scripture wasn't a bad thing. They retreated to solitary rocks in the North Atlantic for no other reason than to find an isolated place in which they could enjoy God's creation and his presence. They connected with a God who animated their lives and enhanced them and seemed to be happy with just that result. The idea of an agenda-less God is a gift the Celts provide to our culture—providing nuances of meaning to the over-used phrase, "desire for relationship."

Perhaps because of my religious roots, I like the phrase "God without an agenda." I think of going for coffee with someone knowing he or she is looking forward to connecting with me more than co-opting me into their plan. Does God have an agenda? Does he have a strong desire to thwart injustice and overcome evil? Didn't Jesus come to the world to destroy the works of the devil? Of course. But does he, in humility, put that agenda aside in deference to his greater agenda? which is to know us? Apparently, yes.

That is astounding.

Think of the Irish age of the saints. Could there have been a time in history when a social agenda would've been more urgent? In the sixth and seventh centuries, civilization had crumbled and there were but a few outposts of reason and faith. Theirs was not a safe world, yet the Irish spent time wandering and getting to know God and were not in a hurry. And, somehow, they still managed to change the world.

God's agenda-less stance motivates me to worship him—and this is not a small thing for someone made immune to worship. For a long time, worship was not my favorite part of church. The music played, and I would stand, sit, occasionally raise my hands, all the while knowing I was missing the real item. I felt like a spectator. The Bible says we love God because he first loved us, but I endured twenty years of worship before someone told me, with enough conviction that I believed him, that God loved me. More than that, God apparently took pleasure in my joy (what father wouldn't?). That knowledge had large repercussions in my ability to worship. The music that made me happy must make God happy. That concept still makes my heart swell. When I hear a worship guitar riff that cycles, resonates, and is played with some intensity, I feel the pleasure of the music and I'm reminded how much God loves me. Feeling his joy shares no common ground with the sense of guilt I used to feel in that situation. In a way that can't be described outside of relationship, he shares my musical taste. God's humility extends so far as to take joy in my simple pleasures. That is mysterious, astounding, and even seems dangerous and draws my heart to him all the more.

Naming

If something is truly new, it lacks a name. To make the new covenant meaningful to us, we need to name it.

Naming and newness go together. In the Genesis account, when Adam first saw the animals, they were all new to him and thus required naming. When we encounter something new, we may not know what the thing is for, how it is to be used, or its relationships with other things. Dr. B. N. Srivastava, a professor of behavioral sciences at the Indian Institute of Management, discusses this process in the paper "The Concept of Newness."[5] He says an exploration generally occurs to find out the unknown things. If the exploration is successful, there is a structural change that occurs in our knowledge and a name results. The name of the thing becomes meaningful, and simultaneously, the thing ceases to be new.

Since, as the road to Emmaus story confirms, much of our experience with Jesus continues to stay new. I'm not sure our naming is ever fully complete. What that means is our journey is rightly personal and always in the process of development. We add pegs of understanding and definition. This is what I believe Paul meant when he wrote, "continue to work out your salvation."[6] He meant explore the work God has done. Own the pegs of your theology; blend them with your life. Make sure they have some history with you. It has to be a solid and positive history, so the pegs can't be borrowed from someone else or transferred from your old story.

One of my pegs is that God is good. Another is that God speaks to everyone. Your new story is a big part of what defines your pegs. Paul to the Galatians (Celts, remember) holds out the standards by which they can define the pegs they hang their theology on:

- the absolute truth of the gospel—the message he preached
- the individual, internal experience that they had—the message they accepted

Paul holds both out in equal measure as valid reference points. He gives authority to their experience and their personal revelation of the new covenant; he gives their experience value while at the same time holding it accountable to the absolute truth.

A question to ask in the naming process is, what were you saved from? Salvation is intensely personal. It always has been. There's something deeply unique about the way each person comes to the end of his own machinations and the way God reaches down and draws him or her out of despair and toward life. What, in the end, would've destroyed you without God's intervention? You can ask, "What was I saved from?" and "What was I saved to? Your answer will help you define your pegs and highlight the unique nature of your spiritual journey. Salvation is an extremely personal thing. Although the foundation of it does not change, it means something unique to each person and each person has to wrestle with their own salvation in their lives. Maybe your life without Jesus was characterized by foolishness and so you desire wisdom, and Jesus directs your journey toward it. Maybe you were saved from pride and your desire at a deep level is for an authentic humility.

These questions will help get to the root of what it means for you to be saved. Where were you before Jesus and how is he now transforming you from that into the creature he intended? This has nothing to do with works or systems; everything to do with dealing in reality and wholeness.

Another of my pegs is the foundational nature of grace. That could likely be your peg too. But they will each have a different perspective to us based on our experience. It's like a different color. The difference may appear minor, but it's critical. The new covenant is not a system, it's a relationship. Your relationship with God is slightly different than mine. To the church in Pergamum the Spirit said, "To him who overcomes I will give some of the hidden manna, and I will give him a white stone, and a new name written on the stone which no one knows but he who receives it."[7] There is a part of our lives with God, both now and beyond, that is deeply personal.

Safety

We earlier saw how the epic Irish myth *The Tain* was filled with tales of battle and bravery. Many themes weave through the saga, but one, I notice, is the theme of fear and foreboding—particularly when the soldiers settle and camp for the night. The soldiers are soothed from this fear by alcohol and merrymaking, but in some descriptions, such as the one following, they don't fare as well.

> And that night Cú Chulainn waved and brandished and shook his weapons so that a hundred warriors among the host died of fright and fear and dread of Cú Chulainn.

I think of this fear as the backdrop to the Irish age of saints. I think of the contrast between the fear evidenced by a company of soldiers expiring because of a sense of dread and the boldness later evidenced by a few Irish saints setting out to wander unregulated territories without a fixed plan.

> In the fullness of their trust leaving themselves to the guidance of the spirit of God.[8]

What seems apparent from that particular facet of Irish transformation is that the new covenant provides relief from a sense of fear. Or perhaps it provides the sense of having a safety net: the ability to live your life inside of the knowledge that you are in your Father's care and outside of the "one strike and you are out" mentality. Living free of fear, whether based in reality or not, is a significant advantage—it releases creativity and all sorts of other faculties. In the new covenant, freedom from fear is more than just a beneficial mental construct; it is a truth we can rely on, regardless of our environment.

Jesus' story of the sheep and the goats best describes why we can be free from fear. When Jesus comes in his glory, he will gather all nations before him and separate the sheep from the goats. How does he separate them? The text doesn't say. Distinguishing physical sheep from physical goats is easy, but we can't easily tell a spiritual sheep from a goat on the outside. You have to know the new covenant to get that knowledge. The sheep know Jesus; the goats don't. It's personal. It's internal.

The good news follows in the story. Look at the difference in the way the two "animals" are judged. Many people think the sheep's actions distinguish them from the goats. Their actions don't distinguish them. If you have any doubt, read it again. The sheep can't lose. They are praised for their smallest effort. Conversely, the goats can't win. They are condemned for their smallest failure. There is a different standard applied to each, and clearly the sheep have the sweet deal. They have a positive bias applied to their lives, and instead of expectancy of judgment, they are faced with unexpected blessings.

The Irish exemplify that however you get to be a sheep, once you become one, you live in freedom from judgment and fear. And it is great news.

Religion

Studying Patrick reveals the extent to which religious forces will go to oppose messengers of the new covenant. The means they employ include slander, public discrediting, amplifying trivial faults, and questioning of credentials. If we expand our field of vision and look at other new-covenant pioneers, Jesus and Paul, we see that their most significant opposing force came from those who enforced and protected religious paradigms, structures, and activities.

We need to recognize the strength of this opposing force to be able to withstand its insidious onslaught. The onslaught comes from both without and within. It comes from within as I find myself quickly morphing the new covenant into a bounded system with rules that coincidentally suit me and my crowd. What sprouts from that deviation is like the cancer that sprouts where the life of the new covenant is absent. God's thoughts are so much more extravagant and so much less petty than mine. My thoughts tempt me to judge and coerce others by manipulation or guilt, which makes me an agent of religion. God's new-covenant thoughts emphasize the value in people and make the people around me too significant, too substantial; too wonderful to judge or control. I may not agree with them. They may even be acting foolishly, but ultimately they require respect as creatures made in God's image with freedom to receive (or reject) God's truth and freedom to exercise the particular authority and significance and manage the responsibility they are given in this age.

The new covenant suggests that my connection with God is primarily, but not exclusively, meant for mutual friendship with him. With this mindset, when I try to fathom God, a respect for the journey within others will keep my knowledge from being subverted into a tool of control. In other words, I will keep far from a controlling and jealous religious mindset.

The religious voice from the outside doesn't bellow, it drones. Its droning communicates that believing in Jesus alone is foolish and naïve and we must additionally improve ourselves. The droning communicates there is not a blank page in front of you—rather there is a complicated system. God is not your loving Father; he is an aloof judge. He does not long to connect with you; he stands back to assess your performance. Religion says there are a lot of expectations for you, little real support, and little possibility of making more of a difference than those before you. For me, this religious message was not communicated in a single abusive event, rather in an insidious ongoing way. That's why I use the word *droning*. For example the placement of a single word—*but*—very effectively works religion's magic. God loves you unconditionally, *but* you must not take advantage of that love. God is your Father, *but* he's a father who wants obedience. You sins are forgiven, *but* you must be truly sorry and not do them again. It's insidious and most definitely leverages the full volume of Scripture. In business I know why a client gives me a voluminous contract. They want to state and restate requirements and create multiple ways to reduce their risk and constrain my behavior. That's conventional religious wisdom—unpacked. It is unassailable, ugly, and sophisticated. It may be the voice of your familial religious institution.

So maybe it is not surprising that God took people who were completely pagan, weak in commerce, used cattle for currency, had no real towns, and fought battles with passion but little plan and set them up as a model for the new covenant. What they lacked in sophistication, they made up for in a preoccupation with otherworldly pursuits, a desire for beauty, and a belief that there was a word of truth at the core of the universe. It is as though God reinforced their lack of sophistication. They reflected the beatitudes—blessed are those who hunger and thirst for righteousness, for they shall be satisfied. In the Irish age of the saints, God seems to have created a blanket of security around their culture in order to incubate their passion for him. They endured pain and hardship, but counted it as joy. Their lack of religion was their asset.

We must recognize that religion is no place for blind trust. Place your loyalty with the Author of your faith and recognize that your own knowledge base and your familial religious institution are not always on your side. You are needy, you are loved; you need a Savior.

In the midst of opposition, whether religious or otherwise, it helps to find a place of healthy focus. The facts about me and the facts about others may temporarily dislodge us from the pursuit of beauty. About me: I'm not pure and unselfish; I'm not very honest about my feelings; I'm not very transparent. The facts about others: they don't spend their time thinking about me; they have little desire to further my life and they often do things to deliberately or coincidentally hurt me. Those realities can easily become a recipe for discouragement and eventual shut-down. The place of healthy focus is a place as wholesome as you desire to be, a place where you won't be dashed to pieces when you take off your armor, a safe environment for your desires to flourish (safe from others and safe from yourself). I find that place in worship where I surrender to God's heart, and I find it in forgiveness: in the experience of God's forgiveness for me (including my contradictions). Jesus' model prayer uses the term "forgive *us* our sins" meaning apply/receive forgiveness at an experiential level. I also find it in the choice to forgive others for their real and perceived aggressions. In fact all these three "places" follow the Celtic example of being people who are marked by "an intense sense of presence."⁹ They are places where we experience and live in God's presence.

Conclusion

THERE ARE TIMES when the features of the new covenant seem so mismatched with the world I live in. Sometimes the distinction between people seems more pronounced than the inclusion Jesus offers. Sometimes people's internal compass seems to point entirely in the wrong direction. Sometimes my world seems polluted with false ideas, and, surprisingly, populated with people hostile to Christ. Paul spoke of those who catch the fragrance of Jesus, but to them it smells of death. How, I wonder, does the relational, internal, inclusive new covenant apply to them? In these times of mismatch I have come to believe the new covenant, with all its implications, is real but not without enemies. Paul describes our primary enemy as "the god of this world," and this god's chosen method of attack is to cause blindness. He blinds minds to the light of the new covenant.[1]

It's not a coincidence that Jesus so often encountered blindness in the gospels. You could say healing physical blindness was symbolic of his ministry. Jesus gave proof to John the Baptist that he was the anticipated new-covenant messenger by saying, "the blind receive sight."[2] Sight still needs to be restored because many still blindly (or illogically) oppose that which brings them life. They either miss the elixir of life altogether or perceive it as death. From this predicament they obviously need release, and Jesus—the Word of truth at the core of the universe—provides the opportunity for that release. He destroys the blindness we suffer under by his Spirit and presence; by releasing a touch of grace, speaking a bold word of truth or offering a word of comfort. This removes the shroud over our eyes, allows us to see and receive the inclusive love he offers.

I, for one, need this kind of help because I don't lunge into new territory as much as I straddle the line of the new. I wrestle with, and sometimes against, new things. I can relate to Copernicus, who waited until he was near death to release his ideas to the public. He knew promoting the sun as the center of the universe was new and dangerous. Our world requires faith, intentionality, and bravery of those who pursue truth.

Yet newness is absolutely critical. For me newness has always indicated the strength of my connection with God. It's the spice and the fruit that follows encounters with God and his spirit. When I stop following the crowd and start receiving His grace; when I surrender my pride and ask for more of His presence, inevitably I find myself with the desire, initiative and courage to embark in new directions. None of these bold traits are inherent to my person. They are God breathed into me—the result of His spirit. He does new things and those new things rub off on me. They keep my life interesting. When I first experienced God, my staid life was jolted by new events. I started a business, started playing ice hockey, got married; had kids. Those new things were uncomfortable then, but now give me joy and keep me sane. So if I find nothing new in my life now, what will keep me sane in five years?

The Irish poets used the term "Christ the ever-young" to describe his eternal nature. The more I read the gospels, the more I see Jesus as a brave and good shepherd who loves and cares for his sheep, but he also uses exciting and youthful words like *new* as a beacon of hope—hope for a better life and a life that leaves a lasting and individual legacy.

I hope you move toward a fuller life as you turn and shed ineffective views of God that are untrue, obsolete, and don't work. I hope we will open the door of discovery so we can recognize the incredible riches of God's kingdom and recognize and treasure each kernel of newness that God brings our way.

For me, the new-covenant theology and rational arguments are like the underbrush to navigate through to get to the land of the new covenant. They are not the new covenant itself. Becoming sure that God is not angry, casting off the religious idols—that is the chainsaw work in the forest. Once that work is done and that trail is fixed, I can live in the mountain meadow of new covenant. The atmosphere there is one of freedom and adventure, and the goal in that place is to live a sort of holy, carefree obedience. There are struggles and opposition but the primary choice is to surrender to the compelling reality of God's presence and to face toward the sun (Son).

You know your journey is pointed in the right direction when you see restored relationships—between yourself and others, and between yourself and God. Remember, God cleared the underbrush for a reason—to get to know you. He is leading you toward an authentic face-to-face relationship with him. When that sinks into your heart, it will change you, and it will change your daily routine. You might take new chances and try new things. You might make time for your son or daughter, to walk with, understand, and honor him or her. You might release control and look into his or her budding adult heart. You might see in their eyes a yearning you've never seen before—a yearning, previously concealed, for connection with their father. The joy you will feel over a hint of that stolen relationship being restored will give you an idea of what your heavenly Father feels and craves. He wants to know you. That one desire presents the only plausible rationale for why he initiated something as uncontrolled as the new covenant. He did it for the joy of reconnecting with his children.

ENDNOTES

Chapter Two

1. Douglas Cardinal QC, "Message in a Building," *PEGG Magazine*, July 2009, vol. 37 no. 7.
2. E. Lhuyd, *Archaeologia Britannica; An account of the languages, histories, and customs of the original inhabitants of Great Britain* (reprinted: Irish University Press, 1971), 290.
3. Nora Chadwick, *The Celts* (New York: Penguin Books, 1971), 46.
4. Ibid.
5. Paul's letter to the Galatians was written in about AD 70 to descendants of those pacified warriors, the first Celtic people to be converted to Christianity.
6. Barry Cunliffe, *The Ancient Celts* (Oxford University Press, 1997), 256.
7. *Patrick's Confession*. In this book all excerpts are taken from the Latin translation by Joseph Duffy in *Patrick In His Own Words* (Dublin: Veritas Publications, 2000).
8. *Táin Bó Cúalnge* from the *Book of Leinster*. All quotes taken from CELT: Corpus of Electronic Texts: a project of University College Cork. College Road, Cork, Ireland.
9. Peter Berresford Ellis, *The Druids* (Grand Rapids, MI: Eerdman's Publishing, 1994), 27.

10. *The Celts,* 54.
11. C. F. Cusack, *The Illustrated History of Ireland* (Hamden, CT: Bracken Books, 1987), 128.
12. Tacitus. *Ann.* xiv. 30.
13. *The Ancient Celts,* 187.
14. *The Celts,* 47.
15. *The Druids,* 167.
16. *The Illustrated History of Ireland,* 55.
17. *The Celts,* 114.
18. Myles Dillon and Nora Chadwick, *The Celtic Realms* (Secaucus NJ: Castle Books, 1967), 97.
19. *The Celts,* 118.
20. *The Celts,* 43.
21. *The Druids,* 113.
22. Thomas Cahill, *How the Irish Saved Civilization* (New York: Nan A. Talise-Doubleday, 1995), 129.
23. Quoted in *The Druids,* 71.
24. *The Celts,* 186.
25. *The Celtic Realms,* 150.
26. From *De Bello Gallico Book VI*, as quoted by Peter Berresford Ellis in *The Druids.*
27. *Táin Bó Cúalnge.*
28. *How the Irish Saved Civilization,* 131.
29. *How the Irish Saved Civilization,* 129.
30. *The Druids,* 140.
31. *Táin Bó Cúalnge.*
32. *Táin Bó Cúalnge.*

Chapter Three

1. Luke 22:20.
2. H. C. Puech, Exposition called "Gnosis and Time" from the EranosYearbooks volume on *Man and Time, 1957.*
3. Robert M. Pirsig, *Zen and the Art of Motorcycle Maintenance* (New York: Bantam, 1981), 7.

Endnotes

Chapter Four

1. The primary teacher in the New Testament is Jesus, as confirmed in John 13:13. Our direct linkage to Jesus is confirmed in passages like Jeremiah 31:34 and Matthew 23:10.

Chapter Five

1. Or were considered to even exist. Consider the statement of Caesar recorded in Luke's gospel to undertake a census of all the inhabited earth. This census certainly did not include the tribes in Ireland and indicates the mindset toward those beyond the scope of Rome's influence.
2. If we place his birth at 385 (though the exact date is uncertain) and some consider it likely he was born fifty years later.
3. *Confession.*
4. Annal M5160 from the Annals of the Four Masters (The Age of the World, 5160), M5160.1.
   "Conaire, son of Ederscel, after having been seventy years in the sovereignty of Irelend, was slain at Bruighean Da Dhearg, by insurgents. It was in the reign of Conaire that the sea annually cast its produce ashore, at Inbhear Colptha. Great abundance of nuts were annually found upon the Boinn Boyne and the Buais during his time. The cattle were without keepers in Ireland in his reign, on account of the greatness of the peace and concord. His reign was not thunder producing or stormy, for the wind did not take a hair off the cattle from the middle of Autumn to the middle of Spring. Little but the trees bent from the greatness of their fruit during his time."
5. *Confession.*
6. This quote and all remaining unnoted chapter quotes are from Patrick's *Confession.*
7. *The Celts,* 206.
8. Joseph Duffy, *Patrick In His Own Words* (Dublin: Veritas Publications, 2000), 52.

Chapter Six

1. Coleman Barks, *The Essential Rumi* (San Francisco: Harper SanFrancisco, 1997), 36.
2. 1 Corinthians 13:5.
3. Henry David Thoreau, *Civil Disobedience*, first published under the title *Resistance to Civil Government* in 1849 in an anthology called *Æsthetic Papers*. This widely read and influential work is readily available on websites such as Project Gutenberg.
4. Matthew 23:16.
5. Matthew 28:20; Hebrews 13:5.
6. Augustine, *Confessions*, book 1, chapter 1.

Chapter Seven

1. Isaiah 54:9.
2. Luke 3:6.
3. Universalism is a belief that all people will ultimately be reconciled to God. I do not hold to it, but the undeniable universal language in new-covenant statements points to the Father's broad desire in our age for relationship with his creation/children.
4. Psalm 94.
5. Jeremiah 8:8: "How can you say, 'We are wise, for we have the law of the LORD,' when actually the lying pen of the scribes has handled it falsely?"
6. Margaret Stokes London, *Three Months in the Forests of France* (George Bell & Sons, 1895); appendix vi gives the list of the first teachers in the seventh century who spread the Columban Rule from Luxeuil in Gaul.
7. *Life of Saint Columba, Founder of Hy.* Written by Adamnan, Ninth Abbot of that Monastery, ed. William Reeves, (Edinburgh: Edmonston and Douglas, 1874, chapter XXIX) as found in the Medieval Sourcebook: a collection of public domain and copy-permitted texts related to medieval and Byzantine history.
8. *The Celts*, 208.

9. By our standards their unorthodox ideas and practices hardly seem scandalous; rejecting clerical celibacy, eating meat during lent. Nevertheless the attitude of the religious establishment toward Celtic characterizations of the faith remains a subtext as the Council of Soissons (744), Ver (755), Mainz (813), and Tours (813) all issued rules and warnings regarding these strolling bishops.
10. Written from the Parknasilla Hotel, Sneem, 18th September 1910.
11. John Macquarrie, *Paths in Spirituality* (SCM Press, 1979), 123.
12. Celtic Realms, 6.

Chapter Eight

1. 1 Samuel 7:4.
2. Matthew 8:22.
3. Luke 14:26.

Chapter Nine

1. Matthew 9:16.
2. Jeremiah 31:34.
3. *The Celts*, 218.
4. He ended up in the Monastery of Saint Peter in Salzburg and by esteem of his peers was raised to Abbot there.
5. D. Chattopadhyay and B.N. Srivastava, B.N., "The Concept of Newness," *Int. J. Management Concepts and Philosophy*, vol. 2, no. 3, 240–245.
6. Philippians 2:12.
7. Revelation 2:17.
8. Dom Louis Gougaud, *Gaelic Pioneers of Christianity* (Dublin: M.H. Hill, 1923), 21.
9. *Paths in Spirituality*, 122. He identifies the key feature of Celtic spirituality as an "intense sense of presence."

Conclusion

1. 2 Corinthians 4:4.
2. Matthew 11:5.

Appendix

A POSTER OF Einstein hung on my wall when I was in university. The caption read, "I want to know God's thoughts, the rest are details." I liked that perspective. With it, Einstein discovered special relativity, seemingly in a moment. Yet he labored for years to work out the details of general relativity. Details always take longer, they raise problems. The devil is in the details, they say. Believing God's ultimate desire is for relationship can be a bit like that—God's heart and thoughts leave a turbulent wake filled with questions and unresolved details. In this appendix we will address some of them.

First, as the poster confirms, details are not the crux of the matter—they are secondary. You perceive the new covenant with your spirit. A child can understand it. Focusing on details indicates something—maybe sophistication, maybe intelligence, maybe sage wisdom but not necessarily that you are following a higher order of things. Details are useful to help process, defend and support new ideas. They can often refine and perfect rough ideas. But they need to be kept in their place—in this case, in the appendix.

And it's also worth noting that some questions are better left unanswered. The new covenant is simultaneously all around us and easy to miss. We need changes of perspective to avoid missing it and once we establish a new viewpoint it's surprising how a word of skepticism can move us, as if on a worn couch, back into the comfortable center and away from that glimpse of the new. Some questions seem to serve only to promote skepticism. Addressing the question, then, does more to support the stance from which the question was asked than provide the requisite answer. It allows the questioner to continue to look past all the new, like it wasn't there.

Nevertheless the following are a few questions raised by various people I have come in contact with in the last few years. My answers are given for the sole purpose of continuing to make God's new deal a little easier to grasp.

"How broad is the new territory Jesus offers?"

    a. Very broad. We have the ability to discover the universe. The freedom God gives us could lead anywhere and represents very broad and unique territory. The outcomes are not all the same, however, and the critical determining factor is connection to Jesus.

"Is the new covenant really the changing of God's mind? Jesus said he didn't come to abolish the Law or the Prophets, but rather to fulfill them. The new replaced the old, because it was better, but does the old really represent a different viewpoint from God?"

    a. To imagine God with a continual, unchanging plan is valid but if that idea is totally true then the word "new" from Jesus is mistaken. God does change his mind in the way he deals with people (Psalm 78) and the single word "new" not only confirms that but provides a refreshing change of posture: like looking at a sculpture from a different angle—one that's not popular and not always permitted but one that is valid and provides some fascinating insight to the work of art.

"Many view the Old Testament as a book full of love. Hosea 11:1-9 is seen, for example, as one of the greatest love passages in the Bible."

    a. Hosea prophesies to the northern kingdom of Israel just before it is overcome by the Assyrians. He speaks of God in the process of change (My heart is turned within me) and, as a prophet, his words anticipate the new covenant.

"Many view the Old Testament as a story of grace. The Ten Commandments start with the reminder that God saved them out of slavery first not because they obeyed any commandments. Exodus 20:2"

    a. There is grace in the Old Testament, certainly, but the primary theme, emphasized by the Prophets and the Minor Prophets is reward for obedience to the law and cursing for disobedience.

"Doesn't the use of the term heretic in Patrick's breastplate presuppose he held an orthodox theology?"

    a. Patrick's language is direct and robust. He's not someone who suffers injustice gladly and was wary of the false laws of heretics. What defined a heretic for Patrick it seems related to pagandom, idolatry and false laws. Nothing in his statement suggests that Patrick was strongly tied to a religious form of thought. Do heretics exist in the new covenant? Certainly, they are those who deny the reality of the age—Jesus. Should we be quick to classify people as heretics—certainly not.

What about problematic scripture verses, examples of which are Matt. 22:36-37, Matt. 28:19, Luke 24:45, Rom. 8:5, Rom. 12:2, Rom. 15:6, 1 Cor. 1:10, 1 Cor. 4:17, 2 Cor. 11:3, Eph. 4:22-24, 1 Tim. 4:11, 1 Tim. 6:2, 2 Tim. 2:24, Titus 2:3, Titus 2:11."

    a. The list consists of verses people have raised to me. Actually I can't see how many of these are problematic. The list in fact seems to reveal how many problems are-subjective—the result of previous false understandings which are likely accompanied by emotional baggage. For those passages that truly appear to be contradictions, as noted in chapter 8, I recommend putting them on the shelf for a period and dwelling on the primary truth of the New Testament.

"Wordless? What about words Jesus spoke, that are recorded in the Bible? What about words Paul spoke that he wrote in the Bible? Things such as qualifications for church office, what to do with the old nature, etc."

    a. Words remain valid. Words in the Bible have recognized authority. However, the foundation on which all valid and powerful words stand, and the direction in which they point, is the new covenant which is essentially wordless.

"I get angry at the injustice and evil in the world. Sometimes anger is appropriate. How can God not be angry?"

    a. Yes, anger is sometimes appropriate. Do a search on the word anger in the Bible. You will see that God was angry, and God does no wrong. But anger was not achieving God's higher goal which is relationship. God is not now angry and we may thus find ourselves angrier than God—which is odd to imagine. It is also odd to imagine the category of specific sins Jesus' sacrifice did not cover and therefore still provoke God's anger. Jesus said, in the new covenant, hating your brother is equivalent to murder. So, given my behaviour, if God is still angry, he must be in a constant state of rage.

CPSIA information can be obtained
at www.ICGtesting.com
Printed in the USA
LVHW11s1945171018
593969LV00001B/18/P

9 781632 691897